Evangelism
and
Contemporary
Theology

EVANGELISM

AND

CONTEMPORARY

THEOLOGY

A Study of the Implications
for Evangelism in the Thoughts
of Six Modern Theologians

PIETER DE JONG

TIDINGS

Materials for Christian Evangelism

1908 Grand Avenue

Nashville, Tennessee

Library of Congress Catalog
Card Number: 62-13349

P

Introduction

*T*he churches of North America have had a quarter century of considerable success in evangelism. They have been enriched by the evangelistic heritage of a previous generation and have learned to use effective modern methods. It is true that their success is being evaluated in widely divergent ways, some respectful and grateful, others sharply critical. Among the latter are a company of social analysts who are bringing everything religious under searching scrutiny, often with unnerving effect.

Whatever may be one's opinion at this point, we may agree that neither the insights of a previous period nor the methodology of our own provides an adequate basis for the outreach of the churches today. We must face basic questions or render our evangelism superficial and unworthy. Our most urgent need is a theology of evangelism.

Undoubtedly, resources are available in the vigorous and vital theologies of our time. But these resources, if available, are not always accessible. A mediator between the theological giants and the practicing minister or layman is needed.

Pieter de Jong is admirably fitted—by background, scholarship, and personality—for this task. A native of Holland and graduate of Amsterdam and Utrecht Universities, he is conversant with the main languages and cultures of Europe. He has his doctorate from Union Theological Seminary, New York, and is married to a former social worker of New York City.

For the past five years Dr. de Jong has lectured in Systematic Theology and Christian Ethics at St. Andrew's College, Saskatoon. He has had extensive contact with church life on the western prairies —a good testing ground for theology, some of us think.

To condense the whole message of six leading contemporary theologians into a chapter each is, of course, an impossible task. But Dr. de Jong has done remarkably well in bringing a central aspect of each theology into clear focus, explaining it, and applying it to the task of evangelism. In the process, the hiatus between content and method that has often existed is bridged: the gospel is seen to have inevitable implications for the Christian's motivation and attitude; and these, in turn, determine method and approach.

The lectures printed here were first given at a Student Christian Movement Conference at Alberta College, Edmonton, next door to historic McDougall Church, an outpost of early Methodism in northern Alberta. They were later delivered to a Conference at Parksville, Vancouver Island, where, in a leisurely oceanside setting, a group of ministers and laymen gathered to consider the practice and propagation of their faith.

I wish that those who read these lectures could have heard them as they were delivered, graced by Dr. de Jong's quiet charm and radiant enthusiasm. Wise judgment and fluent expression were always in happy balance. Contemporary theology was interpreted in a manner that proved of vital interest to both ministers and laymen, and no question failed to receive a satisfactory answer.

Fortunately, the content of the lectures is adequately conveyed by the printed page. The important thing is that Christians should give serious thought to the insights here presented and go on to fulfill the author's hope "that the reader will continue to ask questions along the lines that are developed here and try to find an answer for himself."

G. B. MATHER
Assistant Secretary
Board of Evangelism
and Social Service
United Church of Canada

Foreword

In January, 1961, it was my privilege to attend two Conferences on Evangelism at Parksville, British Columbia. One conference was for pastors; the other, for lay workers. These conferences were held under the auspices of the Board of Evangelism and Social Service of the United Church of Canada.

At both these conferences I heard the lectures of Dr. Pieter de Jong, of St. Andrew's College of Saskatoon, Saskatchewan. From his discussions of "The Evangelism of Present Day Theologians" I received much inspiration and information.

At my request, Dr. de Jong has prepared these messages for publication by the TIDINGS Department of Christian Evangelism. I believe these lectures will have a wide ministry.

Dr. de Jong was born in Holland. He has studied at universities in the United States as well as in his native country.

I bespeak for this book a great ministry of Evangelism.

HARRY DENMAN
General Secretary
The General Board of Evangelism
The Methodist Church

Preface

Somewhere Karl Barth has made the remark that the angels must laugh, first of all about his writing volume after volume about God, as though the knowledge of Almighty God could be contained in a book! But, secondly, they must laugh at the people who write about what Barth, as a theologian, is saying rather than the topics with which he deals in his works.[1]

A book about the implications for evangelism of the thoughts of six contemporary theologians can easily fall under the second category. However, the author, who originally gave these chapters in the form of a lecture series at a conference of the Student Christian Movement and later at a school for evangelism for ministers and laymen, has not aimed merely at reproducing a number of theological thoughts. Rather, his purpose in these chapters is to show that every theology has implications for the communication of the Christian faith. These men compel us to think about the way in which we try to proclaim the good news to the world of our day. They have made the author wonder about this, and all he hopes is that the reader, continuing to ask questions along the lines that are developed here, will try to find an answer for himself.

Dr. Harry Denman requested me to prepare the lectures for publication. He and I are of one mind that evangelism is facing a crisis and that we cannot be content any longer with a mere technique. We need a basis in theology. May these pages do something to bring theology and evangelism closer together.

Those who have helped me in the preparation of these lectures and the manuscript know my gratitude toward them.

PIETER DE JONG
St. Andrew's College
Saskatoon, Canada

Table of Contents

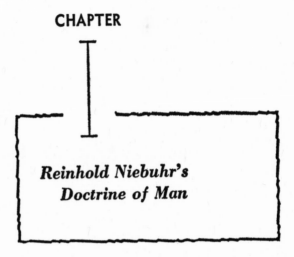

CHAPTER

I

Reinhold Niebuhr's
Doctrine of Man

THE GOSPEL AND THE WHOLE MAN

I

Reinhold Niebuhr's
Doctrine of Man

THE GOSPEL AND THE WHOLE MAN

1

THE GOSPEL
AND THE WHOLE MAN

Reinhold Niebuhr's Doctrine
of Man

MAN: NOTHING BUT A SOUL?

*T*he story is told of a mother who lived in one of the occupied countries during the last World War and who was unable to feed herself and her family. As rations were too small, she went out into the country whenever she had a chance to buy some wheat or some cabbage or some potatoes, depending on what was available. It was toward the end of the war, and the food which farmers were able to sell illegally to people who made demands upon them was usually very little.

One day when the mother was on her way back to town after several unsuccessful attempts to get food, a wagon passed by and some beets fell from its load. She rushed over and tried to grab what she could, but someone else got there at the same time, and the two became involved in a fight. They might have hurt each other badly if a man had not come up and stopped the quarrel. When the woman had finally quieted down, the man looked her in the face and asked: "Has your soul been saved?" Upon which she quipped: "You have not got a soul left when your stomach has been empty for three days!"

"Has your soul been saved?" This is a question which, for many people, is identical with evangelism. But what does it mean? The church, for many, is the institution which is interested in saving souls. But is this the way the Bible puts it? The intention of the man who stopped the fighting women may have been all right. He may have had a point in reminding them of other important things besides food. But the woman had a point, too, when she reminded him that, without any food at all, the soul of a person deteriorates.

We know that people who eat too much can dull their sense for the spiritual. But we also know that people who have nothing to eat are incapable of spiritual interest. The Bible tells us that Jesus came to save people. In saving them, he comforted them. He also healed their sicknesses. How is it possible that the churches, in their evangelistic task, have so frequently forgotten this basic truth that man is a unity of body and soul and that, for this reason, the church is interested in the whole man and not simply in part of his nature?

In his doctrine of man,[2] Reinhold Niebuhr has made clear that the reason for this one-sided interest is the influence of Hellenistic thought which, with the Judeo-Christian tradition, forms the twofold root of our civilization.

The ancient Greeks were known for their interest in sports. Their sculpture shows how they studied the human body with a sense of reverence. They emphasized that the ideal was a healthy mind in a healthy body. Yet they were basically interested in the soul if we look at the great representatives of their philosophy. Idealistic thought, as it developed through the ages, based on the system of Plato, regards the mind of man as essentially good and the body as essentially evil. The Christian Church, in spite of the teachings of the Bible, has often followed this trend and left the impression that, in his mind or soul, man has a spark of the divine and, in his body, a shell which needs to be discarded if he is to come to the fullness of life.

THE WHOLE MAN

A minister was counselling a couple who had shown signs of a strained relationship in their marriage. After some encouragement from their pastor, they had come to see him; and, in the course of the conversation, it finally came out that the two were badly adjusted to each other sexually. The reason appeared to be that both of them had grown up in an environment where sex was frowned upon and therefore never mentioned. They had been brought up in the Christian faith, but their impression throughout had been that the church was fearful regarding any expression of man's sexual function. Sex was something which belonged merely to the body. Faith had to do with the soul. So sex was never mentioned in conversation.

In addition, the impression had been given to them that there was something wrong with a person if he longed for the expression of this aspect of his life. As a consequence, neither of them had ever been able to relate it positively to their life as a whole; and this had caused considerable tension in their relationship. They had thought of mentioning it to their doctor but had been embarrassed about it. The minister was the last person they had considered in this connection; and, if he had not been the type of person to whom you could talk and freely express yourself, they probably would have avoided him in the same way.

"Man is nothing but a soul." Many people in the church think this. Thus, both in their attitude toward the world and in their evangelistic enterprise, they give the impression that this is the message of the Bible. However, they are wrong in this. This is idealism rather than biblical faith.

The mark of idealism, according to Niebuhr, is that it confuses the spirit of man with the Spirit of God and looks upon the body as essentially inferior and evil. Salvation for the idealist means salvation from the body. But in the Bible the whole man, body and soul, has been made by God. If the whole man has gone astray, the whole man is restored in Christ.

SPIRITUALITY

The confusion between idealism and biblical thought becomes

most apparent in the meaning of the word "spiritual." In a discussion group on the meaning of the Christian faith, several of the main topics—like the creation of the world, the sin and salvation of man, the Christian hope—were dealt with in various sessions. When the group discussed the doctrine of God—and, particularly, the doctrine of the Holy Spirit—one of the participants who had been rather quiet during the sessions threw his hands up in the air and said in a desperate tone of voice: "I can't see it. I guess I am not the type. I am not a spiritual person." When he was asked what he meant, he explained that he had gone to church from the time he was a child, that he had been a member of various religious organizations, but that he had always felt he missed something. Those who discussed the things of faith rather freely were spiritual people in his opinion. They must have had this in them from the time they were born, he felt, and must also have had the chance to develop it. He himself did not have it and, therefore, should drop out altogether because he really did not belong.

Spiritual people, we often think, are those who have something of a genius for the divine. They are of a certain kind, just as you are a type which loves sports or appreciates music. If you have it, fine— for you try to develop it; but if not, you had better seek other ways of making life meaningful. Being spiritual, or being religious, seems to be the same for many.

Is this what the Bible means by the spiritual man? The Bible, on the one hand, admits that all human beings have a spirit in the sense of self-transcendence. On the other hand, in speaking about the spiritual man, the Bible does not think of him as someone who has had spirituality of himself from the beginning but as a person who has received it as a gift. The young man who complained about the lack of spirituality was probably closer to the Kingdom than many who claimed "to have it" because they easily confuse their own spiritual nature with the Spirit of God.

"Blessed are the poor in spirit," said our Lord. This literally means: Blessed are those who are beggars with respect to the spirit. The Spirit of God as the Renewer of Man in the Bible is a gift to the whole man, body and soul, and not just the extension of the better part of him. Evangelism, therefore, is not the effort of the church to encourage the good in man or to make him aware of his essential kinship with the divine. Evangelism is rather the effort, under God, to make even spiritual people aware of the need of their whole personality—body and soul—for redemption. The entire man, body and soul, is affected by estrangement from God and needs to be brought back to harmony with the Creator. The gospel is for the whole man.

THE HOLY SPIRIT: CREATOR—REDEEMER

There are at least three aspects of the interpretation of the Christian faith which have been seriously distorted by confusing Christian faith with idealism.

In the first place, if our souls or spirits are basically good and divine, we look upon Christianity as a method of cultivating our better selves. Evangelism in this case is appealing to something in man which is already responding positively in principle. Man's better self may be repressed or hidden, but it is there; and the witness to the faith must try to uncover it and make the other person aware of it.

Evangelism, in this case, presents religion as a method of self-improvement. A person who succeeds in becoming more religious and spiritual has actually helped himself. What we do is ask the divine element in the other person to take life in hand and control it by overcoming all sorts of lower drives in the personality. This divine element is a constituent of his person, and here lies the great difference with biblical thought.

In the Bible the spirit of man is the lamp of the Lord (Proverbs 20:27), but this does not imply that the mind of man is divine. The spirit of man and the Spirit of God come very close to each other, but the basic distinction is always maintained. The Spirit of God is what holds man's life together and remains basically on God's side. He is given from moment to moment. When man dies, God takes back his spirit; and man returns to the earth (Job 33:4; cf. 34:14). We do well to remember that the way in which the story of man's creation is presented in Genesis 2:7 does not suggest a divine spirit as inherent in man's personality.

> Then the Lord God formed man of dust from the ground and breathed into his nostrils the breath of life; and man became a living being.

Human life is constantly held together by the life-giving power of God, but man remains man in the totality of his existence, both body and soul. In the entirety of his life he turns away from God;

7

and, as a whole, he needs to be brought back to the right relationship with his Creator. This, in the Bible, is the work of the Holy Spirit, who is the giver also of new life and of a new heart, as is expressed in Ezekiel 36:26, 27:

> A new heart I will give you, and a new spirit I will put within you: and I will take out of your flesh the heart of stone and give you a heart of flesh. And I will put my Spirit within you, and cause you to walk in my statutes and be careful to observe my ordinances.

Thus the Creator is the same as the Redeemer.

"HEAVEN—CHRISTIANITY"

In the second place, where man's soul is essentially divine, heaven becomes his ultimate goal. For the Greeks, as we have seen, the body is a tomb for the soul (soma-sema). The soul, imprisoned in the flesh, is like a bird in a cage, longing for the moment that the door will be opened and he can fly freely to his destination. To be in the flesh for the soul is a state of estrangement from the original home. Death means liberation. Socrates drank the cup of poison courageously and so lived his creed in front of his pupils. He was not afraid of dying but rather desired it.

Many Christians have read the Bible as though this were part of its teaching.[3] Reading Romans 8:23, which speaks of the redemption of our bodies to which we are looking forward, they understand this to mean the redemption of the soul from the body. But the opposite is true: God made man as a whole, and He saw that what He had made was good. Man's body is also what He had made. Evangelism, therefore, is not simply the effort to get souls into heaven but rather the expression of genuine concern for the whole man. There is no use talking about God to a hungry person if we have the means of providing food. Missionary work often begins with medical care and teaching techniques of agriculture. Christian service is just as much witness as the spoken word even though the word is always needed.

D. T. Niles says that what distinguishes the word from the deed is that it transcends the act. "Our deeds cannot take the place of our word because our word is greater than ourselves." [4] The resurrection of the body for a Christian is something which is experienced in the here and now when all his members are brought into bondage to Christ. It is not something which will be a reality only after we have breathed our last. The gospel is not "pie in the sky." It is healing power for the whole creation. The Bible never gives us the impression that heaven, as a place where men's souls will be happily gathered together, is man's ultimate goal. We may expect the resurrection along with a new heaven and a new earth. Matter is positively evaluated in the Christian faith. It does not need to be denied. But its binding power has been overcome so that it has been restored to its right place in the whole of life.

IMMORTALITY OF THE SOUL AND RESURRECTION

In the third place, when we adhere to the idealistic interpretation of the gospel, we have great difficulty in grasping the meaning of Easter. It is not uncommon to hear the Easter event interpreted as though it were the confirmation of man's belief in the immortality of the soul. The Bible, however, has other things to say. Death is never considered normal, nor is its horrible character disguised. In this respect modern funerals and embalming techniques are in flat contradiction with the realistic manner in which, particularly, the Old Testament looks at the mysteries of life and death. Psalm 115: 17 is characteristic:

> The dead do not praise the Lord,
> nor do any that go down into silence.

Although toward the end of Old Testament days the conviction arose that God would not abandon the dead, it was not until Hellenistic Judaism that the thought of death was made less frightening by teaching that an immortal core of man might survive.[5] For the author of the 90th Psalm, man as a whole comes to an end and faces judgment in being confronted by death:

> Thou turnest man back to dust,
> and sayest, "Turn back, O children of men!"
> For a thousand years in thy sight
> are but as yesterday when it is past,
> or as a watch in the night.
> Thou dost sweep men away; they are like a dream,
> like grass which is renewed in the morning:
> in the morning it flourishes and is renewed;
> in the evening it fades and withers.
> For we are consumed by thy anger;
> by thy wrath we are overwhelmed. . . . (vss. 3-6)

This is the background against which we must read the story of Easter. If the disciples had been convinced that Jesus' soul as the

9

highest part of his nature, was immortal, they would have comforted each other that he was better off after his death than during his life. In his life-time he had been misunderstood and persecuted. Now he was with God and happier because of the fact that his soul was freed from his body and had reached its destination. But this is not at all the case. The stories of Jesus' suffering and death are not accounts of a heroic denial of life. On the contrary. In Gethsemane we see him in agony, and on the cross he cries out his despair as one forsaken by God and men. He experienced the human fear of death; and nothing of this is made weaker by the idea that, after all, it was a way of liberation. The disciples on the road to Emmaus express what all his followers thought: "We had hoped that he was the one to redeem Israel" (Luke 24:21). In other words, if redemption is not taking place in this world and in history, there is no redemption at all.

Easter morning is not the confirmation of what everyone could have guessed, but rather God's unexpected answer—His "yes" to the life of His Son, lived in obedience with body and soul. I Corinthians 2:9 applies to his resurrection as well as to ours:

> What no eye has seen, nor ear heard,
> nor the heart of man conceived,
> what God has prepared for those who love him.

When the apostle speaks in I Corinthians 15 of the risen body as a "spiritual body," he does not mean that only a part of man has come to fulfilment but the entire person's life, lived in unity of body and soul. Life and immortality have been brought to light through the gospel, according to the New Testament (II Timothy 1:10). Only God has immortality of Himself (I Timothy 6:16). This is the Christian hope, and this is what we may stammer about to our fellow men.

MAN: NOTHING BUT A BODY?

The idealist point of view is only one component of modern man's self-understanding. A large group of people with whom we come in contact adhere to the naturalist point of view, which considers man as nothing but a body. While within the church the tendency has been to emphasize the significance of the soul at the expense of the body, outside the church the current attitude is to explain man exclusively from the physical point of view. Niebuhr says:

10

The history of modern culture is the story of a running debate between those who interpret man as reason and those who seek to explain him in terms of his relation to nature.[6]

The naturalist view of man has its roots also in Greek thinking, but in elements which remained subdued in the classical period. While the Renaissance emphasized the role of man as creative along the line of idealism, modern culture is not so much Platonic as it is Stoic and materialistic in its roots.[7]

In a debate between a Christian and a naturalist the origin of man was discussed. The Christian explained how, at times, the church had neglected to emphasize that the biblical story of creation is a symbolic method of expressing the truth that God was at work in the way this world and man came into existence and that He is still at work in it today.

The Bible, he explained, should not be mistaken for a scientific record of facts. Revelation is never a shortcut for scientific inquiry. The Bible does not deal so much with the question "how" as "why." It asks, "From where are you coming, and where are you going?"

The naturalist answered that he was happy that most Christians today see that the scientific explanation of the origin of man is not a sinful pursuit, but that he could not see why man is unique. "Why not," he asked, "admit that man is an animal and nothing more than that? He is born, and he dies, and nobody knows what happens hereafter." In the continuing discussion, he stated rather bluntly: "Is it not a mark of pride that you Christians think so highly of yourselves and of man in general? What gives you the right to say that man is a child of God?"

"Man is nothing but a body." This is the atmosphere in which our secular life is lived. Advertisements and the world of entertainment suggest it and are based on this presupposition. Ideas of love and marriage hardly take into account that man is more than a physical unit. He is considered a bundle of glandular reactions which must be satisfied.

While the church has continued for a long time to act as though love was a matter of the soul only, the current sexual standards, followed both outside the church and within, have become naturalistic. If something is "proved" to be good mammalian behavior, why is it not right? If the majority of people are promiscuous, why should it not be allowed from a moral point of view? Should we not call "normal" and good that which is practiced by most people? Thus we see the tendency to derive moral standards from sheets of statistics. Twentieth-Century man needs a source for his values.

Most people go to their doctor and expect that he can help them with a pill or an injection of some drug. When he is courageous enough to suggest that the cause of the illness, in some cases, may lie deeper and may require a different attitude toward life, or a change in schedule, many look surprised as they do not expect to hear this from a person to whom they have gone in the hope that, with the help of some chemicals, he can restore the harmony of their lives—which, to them, is nothing but the harmony of the body. Our entire lives, including our recreations, seem to suggest that the body is all that counts, and the person who talks of the life of the spirit is considered outdated or strange.

VITALITY

The Bible, however, looks at man as a unity. The Old Testament does not even have a separate word for body. It uses the word flesh, indicating what all human beings are (not have) as perishable creatures (cf. Isaiah 40:6). But there is not the slightest suggestion that the body in itself is evil.

There is a great joy in life. Those who have doubt about this should read that song of Hezekiah which he is said to have written after he was allowed to live on for a while after his illness (Isaiah 38: 9-13; 17-19):

> I said, In the noontide of my days
> I must depart;
> I am consigned to the gates of Sheol
> for the rest of my years.
> I said, I shall not see the Lord
> in the land of the living;
> I shall look upon man no more
> among the inhabitants of the world.
> My dwelling is plucked up and removed from me
> like a shepherd's tent;
> like a weaver I have rolled up my life;
> he cuts me off from the loom;
> from day to night thou dost bring me to an end;
> I cry for help until morning;
> like a lion he breaks all my bones. . . .
>
> Lo, it was for my welfare
> that I had great bitterness;
> but thou hast held back my life
> from the pit of destruction,

for thou hast cast all my sins
behind thy back.
For Sheol cannot thank thee,
death cannot praise thee;
those who go down to the pit cannot hope
for thy faithfulness.
The living, the living, he thanks thee,
as I do this day. . . .

There is not the slightest suggestion that physical life is unimportant. On the contrary, a soul without a body would be—for a Hebrew—like a television or a radio without a loudspeaker.

Christian thought has the same appreciation for life in the body. Every day is received in gratitude as a token of God's favor and a sacrament of His faithfulness. The gospel does not bring the death of the body but rather the fullness of life. And this fullness of life begins in this earthly existence.

According to the Gospel of John, all human beings, of themselves, are estranged from God and live a life which is doomed to death. Vitalism from this point of view is actually the glorification of life which is declining. We are like flowers in a vase: capable of showing strength and beauty for a while, but in reality cut off from the root. True life, therefore, is found only where the link between man and his Creator has been restored and life has become full through the Spirit of God.

MAN AT THE JUNCTURE OF NATURE AND SPIRIT

Man is a child of nature, subject to its vicissitudes, completed by its necessities, driven by its impulses, and confined within the brevity of the years which nature permits its varied forms allowing them some, but not too much, latitude. The other less obvious fact is that man is a spirit who stands outside of nature, life, himself, his reason and the world.[8]

In our evangelistic task we must guard ourselves against the "nothing but" approach which does not do justice to biblical thought nor to honest experience. The idealist closes his eyes to the fact that he is just man and the naturalist to the fact that he is self-transcendent. The author of the Eighth Psalm is, on the one hand, awed by the awareness that God thinks of man at all when he compares himself with the greatness of the rest of creation:

What is man that thou art mindful of him,
and the son of man that thou visitest him? (v. 4)

Man is small and insignificant. Yet, on the other hand, man is called to master the world around him; and, in this sense, he is great:

> Yet thou hast made him a little less than God,
> and dost crown him with glory and honor.
> Thou hast given him dominion over the works of thy hands;
> thou hast put all things under his feet . . . (v. 5)

Actually, the Bible goes farther than that. The contradiction is not merely between greatness and smallness, but also between grandeur and misery. Here, particularly, the Christian view of man collides with either idealism or naturalistic thought. Man is not merely a creature, but a creature in rebellion against his Maker. Therefore, he spends his years as a tale that is told (Psalm 90).

> Either the rational man or the natural man is conceived as essentially good, and it is only necessary for man either to rise from the chaos of nature to the harmony of mind or to descend from the chaos of spirit to the harmony of nature to be saved.[9]

It is Niebuhr's particular merit to have worked out the implications of these secular trends of thought on man's social and political theories. He tests them by the light of the gospel, which has implications also for these fields of human endeavor. Both idealism and naturalism refuse to admit that sin is something which affects man in the very core of his existence and therefore overlook the fact that it cannot be controlled by a mere re-organization. In his very center man needs to be saved. This must be maintained over and against the naturalist who sees him exclusively as a product of nature.

Salvation is not limited to a divine core. This must be asserted before the idealist, who is satisfied with a partial salvation. Sin, according to Niebuhr, is not merely sin of the flesh. It is always spiritual at the same time:

> Man contradicts himself within the terms of his true essence. His essence is free self-determination. His sin is the wrong use of his freedom and its consequent destruction. . . .
> His sin is therefore spiritual and not carnal, though the infection of his rebellion spreads from the spirit to the body and disturbs its harmonies also.[10]

In the New Testament the term "flesh" implies the whole man, with his spiritual and carnal life, living under judgment because of the loss of his right place. Instead of being under God he has made himself like God. Man, says Niebuhr, who is at the juncture of nature and spirit, is marked by freedom and necessity; and this situation forms a temptation: he is inclined to overestimate himself and deny either his spiritual nature or his creatureliness.

THE CHRISTIAN VIEW OF MAN

The Christian view of man should never be presented in such a manner that we give the impression of offering a competing view based on the same presuppositions. We must try to make plain to the idealist and to the naturalist that their points of view are not as rational as they claim. But we cannot proceed from there and try to talk them into accepting the Christian view of man. Only in faith can man admit that his spirit is the spirit of a creature and not divine. Only in faith can man admit that he is not just a child of nature, but also a child of God who is living in rebellion and needs to be brought back to harmony with his Maker. This is not a rational conclusion, but an act of faith on the basis of the incarnation in which God showed that man is of unique value to Him.

We may try to show a naturalist that even his theories regarding man as a child of necessity are the products of a self-transcending spirit; but, in the final analysis, not the mind of man but the Spirit of God convinces a man of the truth of faith. The dialogue with the world, therefore, is a matter of great humility in which the Christian witness can learn a great deal from his opponents.

For the Christian there is no knowledge of man apart from the knowledge of God:

> To understand himself truly means to begin with a faith that he is understood from beyond himself, that he is known and loved of God and must find himself in terms of obedience to the divine will.[11]

Confronted by Christ, man becomes aware of his pride or overestimation of himself which takes on the form of pride of power, pride of knowledge, or pride of virtue. In pride he is more than the victim of ignorance: he disguises his limitations out of fear.[12]

THE NECESSITY OF CONVERSION

Conversion takes place in the core of the human personality and is a matter of grace. Grace is synonymous with the gift of the Holy Spirit, which is not merely the highest development of the human spirit, but the Spirit of God. Niebuhr emphasizes that the indwelling of God's spirit never means a destruction of selfhood. On the one hand, he accepts a degree of compatibility and continuity between

God's Spirit and man's; but, on the other, he always emphasizes that God's Spirit is not the same as man's spirit or identical with its purity and unity on the deepest and highest levels of unconsciousness. "God is not a supernal perfection to which man aspires, but has resources of love, wisdom and power, which come down to man." [13] Without the shattering of the self-centered self man is his own god and will be unable to know the true God.

A wider perspective or enlightenment is not enough. In fact, a wider perspective is merely used in the service of will to power unless man is changed in the core. Speaking of the human heart, he says:

> The necessity of its being shattered at the very center of its being gives perennial validity to the strategy of the evangelistic sects, which seek to induce the crisis of conversion. . . There is of course no absolute necessity for a single crisis. The shattering of the self is a perennial process and occurs in every spiritual experience in which the self is confronted with the claims of God, and becomes conscious of its sinful, self-centered state. . . .[14]

The reconstruction of the self is the work of God's Spirit working in the spirit of man and influencing his natural life also. Although Niebuhr is of the conviction that man, of himself, can become dissatisfied with his own accomplishments and realize the gap between what he is and what he should be, he nevertheless maintains that the spirit of man and the Spirit of God are not related to each other in such a way that the offense of the gospel can ever be evaded. The presence of a point of contact—like the awareness that man is not what he should be—does not imply that faith and reason are in complete continuity. What is foolishness for reason in prospect is wisdom in retrospect for faith. What is weakness becomes strength.[15]

Needless to say, for Niebuhr the discussion with non-believers is far from a merely intellectual pursuit. It is possible only in dependence on the Spirit of God Himself and with the exertion of all powers which He has set at our disposal. Thus, evangelism is a matter of God's grace and human responsibility—a paradox which is incomprehensible from the merely logical point of view, but which has profound meaning for faith.

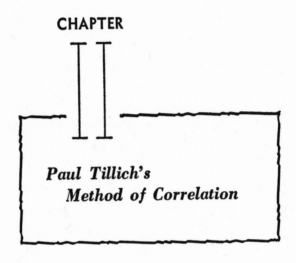

CHAPTER

II

Paul Tillich's
Method of Correlation

THE WORLD ASKS THE QUESTION

FROM THE CHURCH

2

THE WORLD ASKS THE QUESTION
FROM THE CHURCH

*Paul Tillich's Method
of Correlation*

EXISTENTIALISM

A man wanted to break his smoking habit.[16] He had tried all sorts of things; and, at last, he locked himself in an apartment without cigarettes for a week. After he had been there for a while, he discovered a number of cigarette butts, thirty-six altogether. By putting them together, he could make one cigarette out of every six butts. How many cigarettes did he actually smoke?

A non-smoker is inclined to say quickly, "Six, of course." But a smoker, in trying to answer the question, becomes personally involved. He can imagine the longing of this man and live the situation. He will probably come out with the answer, "Seven, because, of the six butts left, he could make another cigarette."

19

This is the difference between detached and existential thinking. Rationalist thought claims to be neutral and impartial. Existential thinking frankly admits involvement. In the first chapter we saw how idealism and naturalism are basically rationalistic. In this chapter we shall deal with existentialism and its implications for the Christian witness.

Existentialism is not a new movement in philosophy.[17] It is as old as Blaise Pascal (1623-1662) who refused to give a logical solution to the problem of man. He was a contemporary of Descartes, who based his philosophy of consciousness on the maxim, "I think, and therefore I am." Over and against this rationalism Pascal spoke of man's greatness and wretchedness in a paradoxical manner.

Sören Kierkegaard lived in the last century (1813-1855) and is called the father of modern existentialism. He was a student of Hegel and rebelled against his philosophy, which considered the world and history the harmonious expression of the divine and universal mind. Existentialism is a reaction against rationalism. Most representatives refuse to call it a philosophy. It is an attitude toward life, they would say.

The word "existentialism" comes from the Latin *existere* which means *to stand out* or *to exist*. In everyday English, the word "outstanding" can have a favorable meaning; but in this case it does not. "To stand out" means "to stand out from original being." It implies estrangement and suffering. Existentialism is aware of the way in which life is threatened every day by destructive and demonic forces. It is frank about the broken character of existence; and, as a philosophy of involvement, it emphasizes the need of living in decision.

Plato, and other philosophers before him, accepted two levels of reality: the essential and the existential. Existence means "being away from one's original home." Therefore, it is painful rather than pleasant, split rather than whole. Throughout the Middle Ages thinkers were aware of this "gap" between what man originally is, or should be, and what he is in fact and reality.

But in the Renaissance this picture changed. Then the "gap" was no longer experienced. Man became the master of the world and of his life. "To exist" was not felt as "being away from home," but rather as "being in one's real element." Man could realize his possibilities, it was believed, to the full in his world; and these possibilities were almost endless.

Here was the beginning of the process of man's emancipation. It was a thrill to be alive and to fulfill one's potentialities. Man was the maker of his world, and a general optimism arose. Existence, says Tillich, was swallowed up by essence. People believed that education and political organization soon would overcome the lag of existence behind essence, and the world would be ideal.

History, according to Hegel, was the process in which this lag was gradually overcome along the way of thesis, antithesis, and synthesis. There were conflicts, indeed, but they were on their way out. Progress became the popular idea. Thus, existence had become the expression of essence rather than the falling away from it.

Thinkers like Nietzsche said that life was not such a peaceful harmony as people wanted to believe. Marx maintained the same of society; Freud, of individual human life. Kierkegaard, with his keen psychological insight, noticed how man is in conflict within himself.

Existentialist philosophy became a protest against a rationalism which had turned man into a tool, into an "it," instead of respecting him as a person. Man, as a result of exploitation, had been pushed around so that life had lost meaning for him. He felt as though he were a mere cog in the machine of organized production and consumption. The truly personal element, the real encounter, had been lost in life; and existentialist thinkers struggled to recover it.

In their effort to find a solution for the problem of dehumanization they went further than stating the problem. Most existentialist philosophers present some answer, and this is usually taken from the tradition in which they stand. Nietzsche was a vitalist and preached the will to power. Marx was a dialectical materialist and preached the class-struggle. Kierkegaard found an answer in the Lutheran tradition; Berdyaev, in Eastern Orthodoxy. Men like Sartre and Camus give a humanist solution to the problem.

Tillich feels that Christians should be acquainted with this movement of thought in our day and age because it states so frankly the need of redemption. They should not necessarily take over the answers provided by these thinkers. Rather, they should ask the question with them and find in the gospel the answer which God has given in His revelation.

EXISTENTIALISM, THE GOOD LUCK
OF TWENTIETH-CENTURY CHRISTIAN THOUGHT

Jean Baptiste Clamence is a successful lawyer in Paris, where he is well liked and glories in his success. He is clever, usually wins his cases, and does not mind when people cannot pay him. He is a man of the world and enjoys the pleasures which the city offers him. Life is smooth, and it seems that there is no limit to his possibilities. He has his mistresses who add color to his life. It is as though he is living in Paradise.

But on a certain evening all this changes. While walking on one the bridges in Paris, he is frightened by the sound of the body of a woman striking the water. He walks on; and, after coming home, he looks into the mirror and sees that he is double-faced.

He cannot stay in Paris any longer. He goes to Amsterdam where he visits the cafes on the waterfront. All he does is talk to people; and the remarkable thing is that, in these conversations, he accuses himself all the time. Pretty soon the people to whom he talks begin to do the same thing; and, after a while, he feels that he can judge everybody speaking to him. It makes him feel superior again, but now in a manner which is totally different from the way he felt on top of things while he lived in Paris.

This, in short, is the content of a novel written by the existentialist author, Albert Camus, who won the Nobel Prize in literature for it. The title of the book is *The Fall*.[18] The Christian who takes up the book, expecting to find in it an exposition of the biblical doctrine of the fall, will be disappointed; and yet, we must ask ourselves: Is there no connection whatever between what Camus says in his book about man and what the Christian faith asserts about him? The connection, as we shall see, is not direct but can only be established indirectly.

The book has a biblical title, and on several pages it has biblical words. It speaks of Eden and has a short passage dealing with Jesus' life and death. It would be wrong to try to identify the "unfallen" state of Clamence with the life of Adam in Paradise. And yet, there is something in this book which is significant for the Christian and which he must appreciate if he wants to communicate the gospel in the Twentieth Century when a number of people think along these lines.

Before his "fall" Clamence is typical of the Renaissance type of man who explores the world and sees no limit to his possibilities. The tragic element in existence is hidden from him. There is no gap, or at least he is not aware of a distance between what he is and what he could be. This changes entirely after his experience on the bridge in Paris. From then on he realizes that there is a split in his life. He has a Janus-face. He pretends to be what he is not. He has a guilty conscience, and it haunts him all over the world. He must escape it, otherwise life is unbearable. The only way in which he can get rid of it or disguise it is to dominate other people. But this does not satisfy him. He feels there must be another way out, but he is incapable of knowing it or discovering it. His life has basically remained self-centered, and the only thing he can do is hope and wait for a time in which these things will be different.

Tillich would call this book "religious" in the sense that it reveals ultimate concern. It poses the question of existence. Man cries out from the depth for an answer. The Christian, in reading it, must not prematurely confuse the Christian terms used in it with the way they occur in works on Christian doctrine. He must first of all learn how to listen to what the author is saying.

THE QUEST FOR FORGIVENESS

One thing which stands out in the book is the cry of Clamence that the acquittal is not heard.[19] The acquittal is not heard in the world; and it is not heard in the church, either. What people have done inside the church, he claims, is to hoist Christ onto the judges' bench and then judge other people.

This is a grave accusation directed to the church. We will do well to listen to it because prophets outside the church have a keen ear for what is going on inside. Clamence is actually doing the same in his world of discontent as Christians do in a religious manner and in a pious environment: judging other people and feeling better because of it. The church, in other words, is not the fellowship of reconciliation, where people accept each other as they know themselves accepted every moment by God.

The author, Camus, is quite right in seeing that here lies the difficulty in Clamence's life: he has not heard of forgiveness, and yet he must face himself and his bad conscience.[20] How can he do this unless someone tells him of his being accepted in spite of the fact that he is unacceptable? It is not enough if someone tells him.

He must experience it as the love of God flows through human channels. Reconciliation is not merely preached. It should also be lived in the church as the fellowship of the reconciled. In their attitude toward the searcher outside, Christians should reflect forgiveness.

What is the advantage of a book like this compared with philosophical writings of a rationalist kind? Tillich maintains that it is the frankness with which the question is asked. Life has become meaningless for many. People do not believe as easily in progress after two World Wars and under the threat of a third. They have a sense of crisis; and this, in some way, makes them ready to listen to the answers the gospel provides. In his booklet, The Courage to Be,[21] Tillich claims that modern man as a whole may not be inclined to listen to sermons on sin, but he knows what we mean by "meaninglessness." He is at a loss in facing life, and the Christian Church should be able to give him what in ancient days the Stoic philosophers did when they helped people in a time of transition with their teachings on courage and resignation. Man in the Twentieth Century needs the courage to face "fallen life." The gospel provides the answer to the quest for meaning, and we should not fail to bring this out wherever people search for it.

Jesus came to seek the lost. He did not come to help the healthy or those who thought they were healthy, but those who were aware of a need. Existentialist philosophy, according to Tillich, is aware of this need. Psychiatry knows about the need of persons for an outlook on life which gives meaning to their existence. Without it, their personality disintegrates.[22] Clamence, after he "fell," was like the sinners and tax-collectors who had no religious pretensions any longer, but with whom Jesus could talk.

Evangelism is nothing else than following Christ in this approach of being open for the question as it arises in people's lives and facing it with them. The Christian witness does not give an answer in those cases, as though he himself is not bothered by the same questions. On the contrary, he feels them in the same way. He, too, is struggling for meaning in life and knows what doubt is.

THE POSITIVE MEANING OF DOUBT

It is Tillich's conviction that the reality of God's presence in our Twentieth Century is frequently felt in the form of doubt. Doubt is a form of ultimate concern in many cases.[23] The person who is engaged in evangelism should be well aware of this. For a long time within the church doubt was looked upon as something of which a person should be ashamed. You did not mention doubt to your minister, and the minister and the evangelist did not mention it to the people. This is an attitude which cannot be maintained in our day and age. The believer, too, knows doubt, not just in the sense of a methodical doubt—as in the field of science—or in the manner of the skeptic, but as existential doubt which is given with his being human. A Christian is a person who knows how to pray: "I believe, help my unbelief!" (Mark 9:24).

If the church were more aware of this, and if we became more understanding of this kind of doubt, our faith would not leave the impression of an easy way out; and we would be more honest in the presentation of the gospel.

THE METHOD OF CORRELATION

The answers implied in the event of revelation are meaningful only in so far as they are in correlation with questions concerning the whole of our existence, with existential questions. . .
Only those who have experienced the tragic ambiguities of our historical existence and have totally questioned the meaning of existence can understand the meaning of what the symbol of the Kingdom of God means. Revelation answers questions which have been asked and always will be asked because they are "we ourselves." [24]

Evangelism can be done only where there is a willingness to enter into a dialogue. The questions are asked by man and by philosophy. But they are not asked in such a manner that the answers which the gospel provides are immediate answers. The answer, to a certain extent, influences the question asked.

Tillich has been frequently attacked on this point; and, in the beginning of the second volume of his *Systematic Theology*, he explains that he is quite well aware that correlation does not mean simple continuity between question and answer. The method requires on the one hand that the Christian witness take seriously the existential situation of his fellow human beings so that he lives in solidarity with them. On the other hand, it means that he is aware of the degree in which the answer found in the gospel determines the question asked.

It should be reaffirmed that the answers cannot be derived from the questions, that the substance of the answers—the revelatory experience—is independent of the questions. But the form of the theological answer is not independent of the form of the existential question.[25]

A simple statement asserting that Christ is the answer to all questions cannot be fruitful in any evangelistic approach unless the Christian witness fully experiences with his partner in conversation the situation from which his question arises. Evangelism requires solidarity. It means entering into other people's lives as Christ entered them in the spirit of compassion and sympathy. It is the opposite of a judging attitude. Rather, it is marked by acceptance of the individual concerned. In that way the Christian witness can become a symbol of the acceptance by God of the person involved.

IS GOD DEAD?

The interesting thing in the life of Clamence is that after his "fall" he had no use for God or religion in any sense. Beforehand, while he was still a successful person, he was not outspokenly religious; but he could at least fit some religious feeling into his life. He felt called to do good to other people even if later on he felt that this was merely a way of boosting his own ego or of buying affection. God, in other words, fitted into his successful life as the one who helped him on the way to his goals. This changed entirely when he had become aware of the ambiguity in his life. From then on he could not stand religion. God had to be thrown out of an existence in which there did not seem to be any sense or meaning.

Tillich tells us how, during the first World War, he and most of the other soldiers in battle agreed with Nietzsche that God had died. Life was not developing in the manner for which they had hoped; and God, who had always been preached as the conclusion of a rational argument, could no longer be a reality to them because the events did not make sense at all. It was not until quite a while later that Tillich found out that it was not God who had died but a certain interpretation of God, namely the idealist one. God was no longer the god in slippers or the kindly man upstairs who was always ready to solve difficult and troublesome situations. He left them in trouble, and it was impossible for most people who had been trained in this kind of Christianity to remain religious in the conventional manner.

Many people whom the Christian witness meets claim that the

God of their fathers has died. They cannot believe what they were told in Sunday school or in church. They have given up ties with organized religion for this reason. The first task in such a case is listening. Is it God who has died, or is it a picture of God which was not a true picture after all and was doomed to break down in times when the tragic element of life had become inescapable for them?

There is no evangelism without apology. We must frankly admit, in some cases, that the church at times has presented the Christian faith as "kid-stuff" which could not possibly be meaningful to people in their later lives except in over-protected circumstances.

EMOTIONALISM VERSUS RATIONALISM

Pascal became convinced of the presence of God in a dramatic experience, a report of which he carried with him during the rest of his life. Some of the words taken from his account are:

> The year of grace 1654, . . .
> From about half past ten in the evening
> until about half past twelve,
> . . . Fire . . .
> God of Abraham, God of Isaac, God of Jacob,
> not of the philosophers and scholars.
> Certitude, certitude, feeling, joy, peace. . . .
> Joy, joy, joy, tears of joy.
> I have been separated from him. . . .
> Let me not be separated from him eternally. . . .[20]

For Pascal, who lived in days when people looked upon faith in God as most reasonable, the awareness of God sprang from a much deeper level than merely the mind. In fact, Pascal went so far as to say that the God Whom he learned to know in his struggles, the Father of our Lord Jesus Christ, had nothing in common with the God of the philosophers Who is the conclusion to an argument. His God was the One Who spoke to the patriarchs.

As an existentialist theologian, Tillich would not go that far. He somehow sees a connection between the question of the philosopher and the God Who spoke through the prophets. But he is convinced that God is not the conclusion to an argument.

A God Whom you can prove is no God. He is an object, and God is never object. The so-called arguments for His existence may have some use. They cannot really convince a person, however, if he has not made a decision in favor of God on a deeper level than his mind. These "proofs" merely point to the question for God raised in human existence. In themselves, they are not sufficient to bring a person to faith.[27]

Man decides in favor of God or against Him neither with only his mind nor with simply his emotions. The danger of an age which reacts against an abstract rationalism is that it easily swings into a superficial emotionalism in which people are worked up into a certain state and then make their decision. Although this may be a true experience in certain cases, we must be careful to realize that emotions separated from the whole of life, or from the center which the Bible calls "the heart," are just as fragmentary as the glorified mind of the rationalist.[28]

Tillich shows how religion has been pushed from the center of man's life into the fringes. Religion has been considered a function of the mind only, and this has led to a sterile faith; or of the emotions alone, which has caused severe distortions in some people's lives; or merely of man's moral function, which has led to moralism.

In none of these cases has it become a vital force, as it was confined to some area of man's life instead of being a choice made in the center.[29] From the heart true faith directs all man's expressions in a wholeness which belongs to the new being. The new being has appeared in Jesus as the Christ who entered our life of estrangement but successfully overcame the gap between essence and existence by remaining faithful to his essential being throughout his earthly life.[30]

Existentialist thinkers are aware of this choice in the core of man's being, even though their decision may be one which leads to a rejection of God. One character in a play by Jean Paul Sartre entitled, Le Diable et le bon Dieu, expresses his joy in discovering that God does not exist in terms quite similar—and obviously chosen to prove the similarity of decision—to those used by Pascal in the account of his experience. He is happy because God is dead and sheds tears of joy for this reason.

In Camus' novel, The Plague, the doctor and the priest stand by the deathbed of a child and neither is able to do anything in order to help him. God does not answer, and life seems absurd.

The Christian witness who will face people who have gone through similar experiences must take their struggles seriously and try to find out which kind of God has died in their lives. Is it, perhaps, an experience which may eventually lead to a deepening of faith, as in the lives of all of us some pictures of God must die when we grow up?

In many cases, the God who died is not the God of the Bible at all, but a god which served as a guarantee of success and happiness. The God of the Bible is the God Who has entered into our estrangement in His Son and suffered with us. The symbol of the Christian faith is the Cross, and the Cross tells us that God did not answer when Jesus uttered the cry of his forsakenness, except in the resurrection. This resurrection was not a usual answer, but one which meant victory in spite of defeat.

ULTIMATE CONCERN AND PRELIMINARY INTERESTS

When you visit a modern campus, the usual picture is that of a group of very impressive buildings. Not only a visitor, but also a first-year student can easily become lost among them and wonder, at times, what ties life in a modern university together. As a rule, the center is the administration building, from which the various departments are directed. In some cases, you see a chapel with its tower rising above the rest of the grounds. But, generally, there seems to be a surprising lack of a center.

Actually, many people do not feel this lack of a center because they have become so accustomed to the situation in which everyone specializes in his own field that the question of how all the different departments constitute a unity has never occurred to them.

This, according to Tillich, is a striking mark of the disintegration of our culture. The wholeness is gone, and people are not even aware of it. Everybody looks at his own field as the most important, and the question of meaning or the quest for truth as a whole is no longer heard.

Here is the student who works hard, but who shows no interest at all if a religious question arises. His only purpose is to get through college as quickly as possible and to obtain his diploma in order to be able to earn some money. If he is asked, "What for?" he shrugs his shoulders. The religious question has disappeared from his life.

Or take the student or the professor who pursues his task religiously. His work and field of interest make up all that counts for him. If the religious question arises, he replies that it is irrelevant to him. His work takes all his time. Actually, what has happened in his life is that a preliminary interest has taken the place of the ultimate concern. His interest has become his religion. His faith has become idolatrous.

When preliminary concerns take the place of our ultimate concern, something essentially conditioned takes the place of the unconditional in our lives.

Most of us are interested in security. We must earn our living, and we need shelter over our heads. The lives of many people, however, are spent in pursuit of only these things. If a reasonable security is reached, success becomes our goal or religion, one might say. In all these cases, the question of ultimate concern is replaced by a secondary interest.

The only right relationship, according to Tillich, is found where our preliminary interests reveal our ultimate concern and are related to it in such a manner that the dimension of depth is present in all that we do. In such a case, religion is not pushed to the fringes of life as in idolatrous faith. Something conditioned has not gained ultimacy for such a person. Rather, his whole life is pervaded by what concerns him ultimately.[31]

LACK OF THE DIMENSION OF DEPTH

Try to take a holiday at a lake, not too far from a city, in order to get some rest. What do you experience? The quietness that you were seeking is hard to find. In the first place, in our densely populated society, it is hard to avoid crowds. In the second place, people cannot enjoy restfulness any longer. Motorboats roar across the water and make swimming a hazard in some places. Man must feel master over nature. Even in his holidays, he must conquer distance by speed —the faster the better, and the more satisfaction he gets out of his holidays!

Man has lost the ability to be by himself and to be impressed by the beauty of nature. He has been brought up in such a way that he cannot feel happy unless he is subjecting it to his will. He has television in his cottage, and on his walks he carries a transistor radio to keep him in contact with the "civilized" world.

The architecture of our modern homes points in the same direction. There is no privacy. Man cannot face himself any longer because he has lost the dimension of depth in his life.

One of Tillich's sermons is called: "Let Us Dare to Have Solitude." In it he tells modern man (who is basically lonely in spite of his physical togetherness with all sorts of people) that the only way to overcome his loneliness is by learning how to have solitude. For in solitude we come to ourselves. In solitude we are not alone. In solitude we learn how to accept our fellow men because we experience our being accepted by God.

What to do about this loss of depth in our lives? Tillich does not have an easy solution to offer:

> The real answer to the question of how to regain the dimension of depth is not given by increased church membership or church attendance, nor by conversion or by healing experiences. But it is given by the awareness that we have lost the decisive dimension of life, the dimension of depth, and that there is no easy way of getting it back. Such awareness is in itself a state of being grasped by that which is symbolized in the term, dimension of depth.[32]

FAITH: A HUMAN POSSIBILITY?

Religion, for Paul Tillich, is an aspect of the human spirit. It is not, as we have seen, a special function of man's spiritual life, but the dimension of depth in all of its functions. This raises the question of the uniqueness of the Christian faith.[33] At a time when the Christian faith is challenged by the encounter with non-Christian religions, this is a question which no Christian may evade.

It is precisely at this point that the weakness of Tillich's position comes out most clearly. It appears that he is more interested in the faith with which we embrace a certain truth than the content of it. In biblical thought these are one. Faith rests on the reliability and faithfulness of God in the Old Testament. Faith in the New Testament is not Christian faith apart from Christ. The Spirit of God brings about true faith and is at the same time its content. The uniqueness of the Christian faith is thus determined by the Christ himself apart from whom man's religion becomes idolatry. Faith as the act with which we receive the Christ is never isolated from God in the manner in which Tillich speaks about the religious dimension of human life.

There are two aspects of his teaching at this point which are difficult to reconcile with biblical thought. In the first place, there is his defense of the superiority of the Christian faith. The Bible, in our opinion, does not speak about the Christian faith as superior compared with other religions. One can speak of superiority only if the difference is a matter of degree. Then, where a faith is claimed to be superior, it is hard to avoid the superiority of the believer. Missionary work has proved both in the past and in the present that the claim of Christianity to be superior cannot be maintained.

31

Even if the superiority, as Tillich claims, is believed to lie in the symbol of the Cross (which actually implies the sacrifice to all claims of ultimacy) we are in a certain sense proud as we feel superior because of our humility.

The second point of weakness appears in Tillich's doctrine of conversion. Conversion, like faith, is determined, not by the content, but by the subjective attitude in Tillich's thought.

> The question of faith is not Moses or Jesus or Mohammed; the question is: Who expresses most adequately one's ultimate concern? [34]

> Conversion also can mean the change from one set of beliefs to another. Conversion in this sense is of no ultimate concern. It might or might not happen. It is important only if, in the new belief, the ultimacy of the ultimate concern is better preserved than in the old belief. If this is the case, the conversion is of great importance. [35]

It is hard to see how, from this point of view, the uniqueness of the Christian faith can be maintained. This is an understanding of faith which neglects the importance of the objective content and must end in syncretism and indifference to the truth of content. Nor can we see how the human spirit in this way of thought is distinguished from the Spirit of God. The divine Spirit here is the fulfillment of the human spirit, and Christian faith is the particular of the human universal. This appears from the following remark:

> Faith in the New Testament is the state of being grasped by the divine Spirit. As Spirit it is the presence of the divine power in the human mind; as holy Spirit it is the Spirit of love, justice and truth. I would not hesitate to call this description of the Spirit the answer to the question and the fulfilment of the dynamics which drive the history of faith. [36]

Does this mean that the method of correlation at this point has failed or is wrongly used in that the question has determined the answer beforehand?

Whether one agrees with Tillich or not on these points, it must be admitted that he has raised questions which are utterly important in the matter of communicating the faith in our day and age. Here and there, as we have seen, the question is asked; but, in order to become the question of faith, nothing less is needed than the Spirit of God Himself as man, left on his own, does not find the answer but remains searching.

Then, there are innumerable cases where the question hardly arises. What to do in such cases? Do we have to sit and wait until a crisis occurs in those lives? Or do we have to analyze these people so that they become aware that they, too, are asking the question? Is this possible?

Tillich's method needs careful examination and application and is not applicable in all cases. There are instances in which we shall need another approach.

CHAPTER

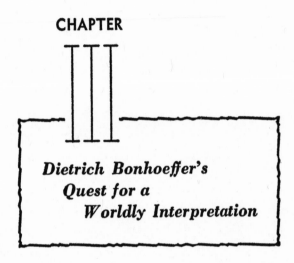

III

Dietrich Bonhoeffer's
Quest for a
Worldly Interpretation

THE CHURCH MUST ASK THE QUESTION
FROM THE WORLD

3

THE CHURCH MUST ASK THE QUESTION FROM THE WORLD

Dietrich Bonhoeffer's Quest for a Worldly Interpretation

WHO ASKS THE QUESTION?

*W*e had a discussion group composed of people who are interested in the faith but not associated with any form of organized religion. One evening, after we had discussed Tillich's approach and examined his method of correlation, one of the participants (a psychiatrist) said: "But do we ask the question? I am busy the whole day, from the time I go to work in the morning until I return home in the evening. After supper I sometimes have a meeting, and otherwise I do some work at home. I have a wife and children whom I love. If people come to me at my consulting hour and are too upset about a certain thing, I try to explain to them that they have to become mature and realize that shocking experiences come with life and are part of the bargain. Everybody has them, and we have to learn to take them in our stride if we want to be grown-up. I don't agree with Tillich that all of us are asking the question and going through a crisis all the time. I am one who is not."

Dietrich Bonhoeffer was of the conviction that the time has come when fewer and fewer people ask the question and when, if they ask it at all, they will likely do so in situations at the borderline of life. If we act as though this is the only opportune moment for the evangelist to take hold of things, we are giving in to a misconception, namely, that faith is relevant only when man is at his wit's end. The gospel has something to say in the midst of life and not just at the fringes.

This would be a religious approach in which we use God, while the real approach is one in which God stands in the center rather than we ourselves. Therefore, we must not wait until the world asks the question from us. This may not happen any more. Rather, we must face them with the question right there where the world claims to be most secure and where the world is at the same time most lonely, namely, in the midst of a situation where God is no longer needed as a pious veneer or as an easy way out.

God must become a reality in the things we know and in the things we like as well as in the times of distress and disaster. The church stands in the center of the town! This is the symbol of a truth which has disappeared from many lives, and we must restore it by confronting people with the question of meaning when they no longer ask it themselves.

Somehow this idea, also advanced by Helmuth Thielicke,[37] gradually ripened in Bonhoeffer's mind after a development in which he began within the church. His dissertation [38] was on "The Church as the Fellowship of the Saints" (which is nevertheless a congregation of human beings). All kinds of sociological factors play a role in its life, and Bonhoeffer was interested in the question of how the work of the Holy Spirit is related to these.

Bonhoeffer was an outgoing type of person and could not remain confined in his interests to the Christians alone. He loved life in its manifold expressions,[39] and his attention was gradually drawn to the outside world as the area in which the church is called to pro-

claim God's kingly rule.[40] In addition, after he had become involved
in underground work during the war, he came into contact with
many secular types of people whom he genuinely liked but about
whose godless outlook on life he was profoundly disturbed. He knew
that this posed tremendous questions to the church in her theology
and her evangelistic approach. What did it mean? Had the role
of the church come to an end? Can we continue to preach the gospel
as the answer to a felt need? Or have people outgrown such an approach? If so, how can we interpret the gospel to them? Do we
demand from them that they return to their former attitude of fear
and lack of ability to face life on their own? Or is there another
approach?

While in prison he noticed how, during air raids, many who
claimed to be Christians were restless and insecure while those who
claimed to have no religion at all faced the experience with surprising
courage. The same took place in the forces and in the concentration
camps where people continually lived under the threat of death.

Bonhoeffer's remarks are worth noting in connection with our
evangelistic approach. One of the factors which keep the church
from an adequate witness in the outside world is an overconcern with
itself. We have become introverts, religiously speaking. If people
challenge us with the question whether God really means something
in our lives, our answer is often something like: "Look at the church
we have built!" Or: "Don't you know the number of religious organizations I attend (or run)?" What we are doing, actually, is pat-
ting ourselves on the back because we think that we are pretty
good Christians when we have built monuments to our own glory
and the memory of God.

As ministers we think that we have done our work if we have kept
the ecclesiastical machinery lubricated so that the members of our
congregations can continue doing their chores. But is this ministry
in the true sense? Ministry always means at the same time ministry
in the world. Ministry—also of the laity—means sharing my faith
with those people with whom I work and play or with whom I live.

Our world has become a godless world. In that respect the world
is suffering temptation. Temptation, according to Bonhoeffer,[41]
should not be understood primarily as testing one's moral strength.
It is abandonment. God leaves us to ourselves. And nobody can
stand this.

This is what happened to Adam in Paradise, and he fell. It happened to Jesus in the wilderness, but he remained standing.[42] It happened to him on the Cross when he cried out: "My God, my God, why hast thou forsaken me?" But Easter morning revealed that he was still with God.

Christians and the world alike go through this abandonment. The church tries to escape it by religion, but she should not. She should rather stand in solidarity with the world, even as God Himself went through it in Christ. The church as the Body of Christ must stand where the world stands and share this forsakenness, remaining obedient as the Son did.

The forsakenness of the world has been taken upon Himself by God and must be taken upon herself by the church which participates in the life, death, and resurrection of Christ. As the Christ, so the church learns obedience through what she suffers (Hebrews 5:8). As the Christ raised the question for us on the Cross as to why God has forsaken us, so the church in the Twentieth Century must raise it for and with the world to show how God is with us in this abandonment. He is not a God who appears only on the outside of life. Rather, He is right there where we have lost awareness of His presence, where everything seems to contradict His relevance and to "prove" His absence.

A WORLD COME OF AGE

What has happened is that the situation in our day and age seems quite different from that of even the last century, when people considered being a religious person something of which to be proud—or certainly not something of which to be ashamed. The world, according to Bonhoeffer in his *Letters and Papers from Prison*, has come of age.

> The movement beginning about the thirteenth century . . . towards the autonomy of man (under which head I place the discovery of the laws by which the world lives and manages in science, social and political affairs, art, ethics and religion) has in our time reached a certain completion. Man has learned to cope with all questions of importance without recourse to God as a working hypothesis.[43]

> . . . it is becoming evident that everything gets along without "God," and just as well as before. As in the scientific field, so in human affairs generally, what we call "God" is being more and more edged out of life, losing more and more ground."[44]

What has been the Christians' reaction to this state of affairs? asks Bonhoeffer. Have they realized it or escaped facing it? They have seen it but reacted against it in a manner which betrayed their fears rather than expressed their faith.

> Christian apologetic has taken the most varying forms of opposition to this self-assurance. Efforts are made to prove to a world thus come of age that it cannot live without the tutelage of "God." [45]

Bonhoeffer reproached the churches for following existentialists who try to induce a spirit of despair without giving an answer or solution. They try to frighten people by reminding them of the ultimate questions, like guilt and death. What are they going to do about these? Don't they need a "God" to solve these problems? So do the psychotherapists who try to prove to people who are outwardly not in too bad mental shape that, in reality, they, too, are miserable and unhappy.[46] The world engages in these two modern trends in an effort to make people despair; but it is not impossible, says Bonhoeffer, that people will learn to solve even these ultimate questions without God. We must face the fact that "God" has been edged out of life. And in times of peace, who thinks of ultimate questions?

> The ordinary man who spends his everyday life at work, and with his family, and of course with all kinds of hobbies and other interests too, is not affected. He has neither time nor inclination for thinking about his intellectual despair and regarding his modest share of happiness as a trial, a trouble or a disaster.[47]

Bonhoeffer touches a very important point. It is a fact which all of us have experienced in our evangelistic approach, namely, that only a certain number of people can be reached by the method which takes into account the existentialist philosophers. If the church does not realize this and does not go out and face other people with the question of forsakenness in an outgoing manner, they will not be reached. God must become a reality in ordinary life, not just in borderline situations.

The mistake which the churches have made, according to Bonhoeffer, in trying to bring people back to religion is that of forcing them into adolescence. A world come of age is asked by the church to act as if it were growing up again, instead of being recognized as people who have come of age and have reached a degree of mental maturity. They are asked to become afraid again in order to make place for religion in their lives when they have just succeeded in facing many a danger without fear and without the need of a pacifying religion.

This is an absolutely wrong method. The question today is Christ and the newly matured world.

It is useless to try to clear a space for religion in our world today. We must find ways and means to interpret Christ without the need of a religious setting. We must stop worrying about the lack of religiosity because religiosity is perhaps not at all such a favorable condition for accepting Christ! And here Bonhoeffer draws a parallel with the people in Jesus' day.

Jesus had the hardest time with the religious people: the Pharisees who were proud of their religious and moral achievements but who, in their pride about their own religion, had no eye for the revealed truth in Christ. On the other hand there were the simple people of the land, the "am haaretz," who either did not have the education or the time or the means to do much studying in the law and the sacred writings. They had no pretensions and were despised by the cultured Pharisees. They followed Jesus precisely because Jesus could have contact with them.

If we were to characterize Bonhoeffer's approach with a word from the Gospels, we would choose the first beatitude: "Blessed are the poor in spirit, for theirs is the Kingdom of Heaven." We understand this statement to mean: "Blessed are those who are not filled to such an extent with the accomplishments of their own spirit and the pride about achievements of their own mind that no place is left for the Spirit of God."

Modern man may be irreligious; but he is honest, painfully honest, in that he forces many a churchman to get rid of his mask. In this respect he is close to the Kingdom.[48]

It is Bonhoeffer's merit to have pointed to this characteristic of modern man. The believers' and witnesses' task is not necessarily to tell man that he is lonely and abandoned, but, as Christ did, to share his abandonment, standing at his side, looking at it from the perspective of faith.

USING GOD AS A STOPGAP

Why is Bonhoeffer so relatively quiet and at peace about the fact that this world seems to get along fine without God? Does it not worry him in the least? Does it not frighten him that the theologian might be put out of business in a short time? No, because the Bible requires faith and not religiosity. Religiosity is a form of escape for Bonhoeffer. Just as people in earlier days used magic to get rid of disease and uncomfortable situations, and now use scientific means, so religion is often used for "salvation" from unpleasant circumstances and even within the church appraised as such. This is giving in to the childhood stage.

> Salvation means salvation from cares and need, from fears and longing, from sin and death into a better world beyond the grave. But is this really the distinctive feature of Christianity as proclaimed in the Gospels and St. Paul? I am sure it is not. The difference between the Christian hope of resurrection and a mythological hope is that the Christian hope sends a man back to his life on earth in a wholly new way. . . . Myths of salvation arise from human experiences of the boundary situation. Christ takes hold in the centre of his life.[49]

What Christianity has often done is to use God as a means of escape from situations for which even the Christian faith does not offer a solution. Faith in Christ does not guarantee a person that he will be a success or that he will escape serious disease or death. It is not an escape mechanism.[50] Freud laid his finger on a sore point when he reproached Christians on the ground that they had invented an ideal father because their earthly fathers were hard to get along with and a heavenly brother because relatives and human beings in general contradicted them. This heavenly brother always agreed with them, and this agreement was an easy way out for many. This type of religion has nothing to do with the Christian faith which requires obedience and sacrifice.

And how often is God used as a stopgap when our human knowledge gives out? Insurance policies are an example of this. In small letters on the back we read that there are certain unpredictable happenings which cannot be covered. These events are kindly—or unkindly—called "acts of God." This wording expresses the conviction that modern man has pretty well succeeded in controlling the hazards of nature but that there are still a few exceptions, and these are called "acts of God." God comes in when we are at the end of our tether.

The same has been done with respect to scientific research. Christians often have talked and acted as though scientific research were a threat. Then, after some time, when the results simply had to be taken into account, there was a yielding in the sense that God was merely pushed a little further to the fringes of life. In other words, Christians gave in to the misconception of much popular science that those things which happen and whose regularity can be traced have nothing to do with God. God is there only where our knowledge gives out and where we have not (yet?) succeeded in gaining exact knowledge.

We have done this with the doctrine of the creation of the world. We have done this with medicine and with many other fields, like space explorations. God is getting farther and farther away until eventually there is no place left.

But God is not a stopgap. He is not the question mark at the end of our knowledge. If this were so, He would be like the answer to a question or to a problem. He is a mystery. And a mystery needs to be revealed and remains a mystery after revelation.[51]

God is the mystery in the center of those events and occurrences of which we think we know all. There is no use for our evangelistic enterprise to demand of people that they make a place for God somewhere at the fringes of their lives. He is there all the time in the center if they only will see it and admit it. The best Christian witness therefore is a life lived with God in the center because words are not enough. I quote Bonhoeffer himself on this problem:

> We should find God in what we do know, not in what we don't; not in outstanding problems, but in those we have already solved. This is true not only for the relation between Christianity and science, but also for wider human problems such as guilt, suffering and death. . . (p. 142)
> We must not wait until we are at the end of our tether: he must be found at the centre of life: in life, and not only in death; in health and vigour, and not only in suffering; in activity, and not only in sin. . . Christ is the centre of life, and in no sense did he come to answer our unsolved problems.[52]

CHEAP GRACE

Bonhoeffer, who grew up and lived in Germany where the Lutheran doctrine of justification by faith was preached and accepted, had much trouble in accepting many of the forms of Protestantism on the American Continent.[53] He called it a Protestantism without the Reformation. While, on the one hand, he objected to any form of Pelagianism—the teaching that God and man have equal shares in the work of salvation—he also vigorously objected to a frequent misuse of the doctrine of justification that conceived it as an excuse from obedience.

In his book, *The Cost of Discipleship*, Bonhoeffer stresses obedience as a consequence of faith.[54] It is not a means of earning one's salvation, nor imitation in the sense of Thomas à Kempis. It is participation in the new humanity of Jesus, which was a humanity lived under the Cross. Bonhoeffer felt that one of the severest diseases of the Protestant Church was a complacent attitude that all was right as long as a person was forgiven. In other words, he emphasized sanctification, not separated from, but immediately following from and being one with justification.

This is an important point for the evangelistic approach. It is amazing how many people there are who are willing to accept the church for the benefit of the community and who want to send their children to a Sunday school because they do not like to see them grow up like pagans. All this is miles apart from real discipleship and sacrificial obedience.

"When Christ calls a man, he bids him come and die." [55] These words became flesh in Bonhoeffer's own life when, after an imprisonment of several years, he was executed in April, 1945. The Sunday after Easter of that year Bonhoeffer was asked to lead a short service of worship for his fellow prisoners in a concentration camp. Many of the prisoners were aware of the possibility that any moment they might meet their end. Bonhoeffer spoke on two verses: Isaiah 53:5: "With his wounds we are healed," and I Peter 1:3: "Blessed be the God and Father of our Lord Jesus Christ. By his great mercy we have been born anew to a living hope through the resurrection of Jesus Christ from the dead."

> He hardly finished his last prayer when the door was opened and two evil-looking men in civilian clothes came in and said: "Prisoner Bonhoeffer, get ready to come with us." Those words "Come with us," for all prisoners they had come to mean only one thing—the scaffold. We bade him goodbye—he drew me aside—"This is the end," he said, "For me the beginning of life, . . ." Next day, at Flossenburg, he was hanged! [56]

WORLDLINESS

Bonhoeffer read a great deal in the Old Testament during his imprisonment, and an intensive study of it in comparison with the New made it clear to him that too often Christians have been other-worldly in the sense of escaping ordinary life. They have been thinking of religion as something which required a "spiritual" attitude in which an other world was a reality. The Old Testament, he found,

45

never escaped from this world into another one; and the New does not do it as much as later Christians thought it did.

Christians have always preached the Christ in a manner which presupposed man's religious nature and attitude. If one happened not to be the type, there was not much that could be done. In fact, some presented it in such a way that people first had to become religious before they could accept Christ. This, says Bonhoeffer, is a great mistake. Jesus appealed to the non-religious people of his day.

> How do we speak of God without religion, i.e., without the temporally-influenced presuppositions of metaphysics, inwardness, and so on? How do we speak . . . in secular fashion of God? In what way are we in a religionless and secular sense Christians, in what way are we the Ekklesia, "those who are called forth," not conceiving of ourselves religiously as specially favoured, but as wholly belonging to the world?[57]

Bonhoeffer was convinced that we are heading for a time of no religion at all. One can debate whether he was right in view of a contemporary revival of religious interest, e.g., in the Eastern religions.

> Our whole nineteen-hundred-year-old Christian preaching and theology rests upon the "religious premise" of man. What we call Christianity has always been a pattern—perhaps a true pattern—of religion. But if one day it becomes apparent that this a priori "premise" simply does not exist, but was a historical and temporary form of human self-expression, i.e., if we really reach the stage of being radically without religion—and I think this is more or less the case already, else how is it, for instance, that this war, unlike any of those before it, is not calling forth any "religious" reaction?—what does that mean for "Christianity"? [58]

Preaching Christianity in such a way that we first try to make people religious is an action parallel to that of the Jews in Paul's day who wanted the Gentiles to become circumcised before accepting Christ. Evangelism should never have a forced character or be done out of fear. We will act out of fear if our own "religion" is based on fear. The best kind of witness is given by standing in solidarity with other people—non-religious, non-Christian people—and by accepting them as Christ accepted them.

Here, again, Bonhoeffer, the theologian, seems to aim at what he would say later, namely, that theological phrases and convictions do not move a person to faith. The best and profoundest Christian witness is given by a life lived in obedience and, at the same time, in complete solidarity.

Is that not what Christ did? Bonhoeffer describes the experience many of us go through in our contact with non-Christians when we find out that often they are open for the Christ because of their lack of "religious" opinions:

> I often ask myself why a Christian instinct draws me more to the religionless than to the religious, by which I mean not with any intention of evangelizing them, but rather, I might almost say, in "brotherhood." While I often shrink with religious people from speaking of God by name—because that name somehow seems to me here not to ring true, and I strike myself as rather dishonest (it is especially bad when others start talking in religious jargon: then I dry up completely and feel somehow oppressed and ill at ease)—with people who have no religion I am able on occasion to speak of God quite openly and as it were naturally. Religious people speak of God when human perception is (often just from laziness) at an end, or human resources fail: it is really always the Deus ex machina they call to their aid, either for the so-called solving of insoluble problems or as support in human failure —always, that is to say, helping out human weakness or on the borders of human existence.[59]

Bonhoeffer is talking about an attitude on the part of many Christians which is easily discovered by the non-believer and which does untold harm to the spreading of the Christian faith. Every person who feels the urge to evangelize must examine himself carefully to see whether, in his zeal and effort, he is making this great mistake of presenting God as the question mark at the end of our knowledge.[60] He must also allow non-Christians to tell him if he errs and be willing to learn from them.

This is one of the most important points in the evangelistic task. Nobody is ever wholly ready for it. Nobody is adequately prepared. However, one of the most important requirements is openness of mind in our contact with non-Christians because many a Christian witness has become stronger in faith by discovering in his discussion with non-believers where he himself was not presenting or living the faith in the right way. We must never confuse real faith in Christ with piety or mere inwardness:

> The discovery of inwardness, so-called, derives from the Renaissance, from Petrarch perhaps. The "heart" in the biblical sense is not the inward life, but the whole man in relation to God.[61]

Here Bonhoeffer touches the question about the meaning of man's spirit in relation to God's Spirit. The human spirit is never isolated from the whole of human life. Therefore the idea of "spirituality" as we find it in our Western civilization is confusing if it is understood as a special quality possessed by some which makes them ready for their contact with God.

"Blessed are the poor in spirit!" Here Bonhoeffer stands diametrically opposed to many a theologian of the past and of the present, but his opposition is based on biblical grounds. He certainly did not deny cultural expressions of man's mind, but he refused to call them a preparation for faith. On the contrary, he was quite well aware of their being capable of keeping man apart from God and acting as a substitute for faith.

The best "worldly" interpretation Bonhoeffer has given of the Christian faith is in his own obedience unto death. A Christian is not a man who simply talks about God but one who stands by God in His suffering with the world.[62] This is his emphasis on participation in Christ's life and death and resurrection—something which does not take place after man's death, but right here and now in this world. Christians watch with Christ in Gethsemane.

It is interesting to compare Bonhoeffer's thoughts on discipleship with Thomas à Kempis' ideas on the imitation. Where for à Kempis faith led a man into isolation and seclusion, for Bonhoeffer it meant that a Christian is thrown back from his habitual secret prayer life into the world.

> He must therefore plunge himself into the life of a godless world, without attempting to gloss over its ungodliness with a veneer of religion or trying to transfigure it. He must live a "worldly" life and so participate in the suffering of God. . . . To be a Christian does not mean to be religious in a particular way, to cultivate a particular way of ascetism (as a sinner, a penitent or a saint), but to be a man. It is not some religious act which makes a Christian what he is, but participation in the suffering of God in the life of the world.[63]

A Christian is an ordinary man who has given up all pretensions and takes life as it comes, always living it in the perspective of the resurrection. By worldliness Bonhoeffer does not mean "the shallow this-worldliness of the enlightened, of the busy, the comfortable or the lascivious." [64] He is thinking of the new life which breaks through where Christ is born in a person; it is a worldliness which knows of dying and rising again: "something in which the knowledge of death and resurrection is ever present." [65]

Conversion for Bonhoeffer means the leading of a life fully in this world but from this new perspective:

I remember talking to a young French pastor at A. thirteen years ago. We were discussing what our real purpose was in life. He said he would like to become a saint. I think it is quite likely he did become one. At the time I was very much impressed, though I disagreed with him, and said I should prefer to have faith, or words to that effect. . . .
Later I discovered and am still discovering up to this very moment that it is only by living completely in this world that one learns to believe. One must abandon every attempt to make something of oneself, whether it be a saint, a converted sinner, a churchman (the priestly type, so-called!) a righteous man or an unrighteous one, a sick man or a healthy one. This is what I mean by worldliness—taking life in one's stride, with all its duties and problems, its successes and failures, its experiences and helplessness. It is in such a life that we throw ourselves utterly in the arms of God and participate in his sufferings in the world and watch with Christ in Gethsemane. That is faith, that is metanoia, and that is what makes a man a Christian.[66]

THE LIFE OF FELLOWSHIP

We are told that the early Christians gained so many converts because of the life they lived together. "Behold, how they love one another," the outsiders used to say. One of the powerful factors in evangelism is perhaps the actual service of worship with the congregation in the act of adoration. In addition, what the world needs most is to see true fellowship lived. The word "togetherness" has become filled with too much of a trivial meaning to indicate what the Bible calls "koinonia." But this is the answer to the basic loneliness felt by most people today. It is not at all the increase of organizations.

Are we moving towards an age of colossal organizations and collective institutions, or will the desire of multitudes for small, manageable, personal relationships be satisfied?[67]

Bonhoeffer's book, Life Together,[68] describes the character of true Christian fellowship. The meditations in this booklet are the fruit of his experience as the leader of illegal seminaries of the Confessing Church, where the men lived together and prepared themselves for the ministry in difficult times.[69] The core of the book is the doctrine of forgiveness. There is no possibility of true fellowship in the profound sense of the word unless we accept each other as we are. We can do this because we know ourselves accepted by Christ just as we are.

This is also the basis of the attitude of the pastor toward his congregation and of the congregation with respect to each other and the world around. The study deals with the character of private devotions and prayers of the fellowship together. Bonhoeffer stressed strongly the need for worldliness, but he also emphasized the necessity of a secret discipline. We cannot serve in the world without our moments in solitude:

> Let him who cannot be alone beware of community. He will only do harm to himself and to the community. Alone you stood before God when he called you; alone you had to answer that call; alone you had to struggle and pray. . . .[70]

Here Bonhoeffer shows where modern life is most lacking. Our ways of being together with others are usually on a level which implies an escape from self instead of the fruit of a life in togetherness with God. A person who runs away from himself into a group is actually using other people for the sake of diversion. He does not want community, which is his deepest need, but rather distraction. A Christian is always an individual; and, as an individual, he is a member of the fellowship.

There is a growing stress on the fellowship in the church today. We have rediscovered the significance of the covenant-community and the emphasis of the Old and New Testaments on the inter-human relationships of man, who is called to serve God. We have come to realize that the Christian who reads his Bible by himself and who says his prayers does so as a member of the fellowship, even if he is by himself.

Jesus taught the disciples to begin their prayer with the words: "Our Father. . . ." A human being is always and acts always as a member and representative of the community. All these truths should not keep us from realizing the extreme need for the rediscovery of the secret discipline in the life of the Christian. This cannot be done in isolation. In fact, just as private devotion should aim at going out into the world, so the life in fellowship with others should lead us to the ability to face ourselves and God in solitude.

> Let him who is not in community beware of being alone. Into the community you were called, the call was not meant for you alone; in the community of the called you bear your cross, you struggle, you pray. You are not alone, even in death, and on the Last Day you will be a member of the great congregation of Jesus Christ.[71]

It is useless to ask the question which comes first, solitude or community. Both begin with and in the call of Christ, according to Bonhoeffer. This outlook influences our speech and our ability to be silent at times. "Right speech comes out of silence, and right silence comes out of speech." [72] We should exercise the ministry of holding our tongues at times, something which many of us, particularly ministers, have great difficulty in learning. The ability to listen is just as important as the ability to speak!

Bonhoeffer reminds all pastors to set aside a regular hour for scripture reading, meditation, and prayer. He says profound things about the way in which we can use the Book of Psalms for private and public devotions.[73] The right use of this prayer book of Jesus and of the Christian Church requires a Christo-centric theology.

In speaking about the ministry Bonhoeffer says a great many things which are not simply useful for the pastor but also for the layman who wants to be a Christian witness. After all, the real ministry is performed by the laity in the world. So they, too, can benefit as the people of God who are called to be witnesses in this world by the way in which they live together as a fellowship of reconciliation.

Perhaps one of the reasons that we feel so restless in the evangelistic enterprise is that we try to compensate the lack of real togetherness among those who claim to be members of the body of Christ. Is it not true that much of the work done by the Church today could just as well be accomplished by a secular organization? What sets the fellowship of reconciliation apart is precisely this element of community which is a fruit of the Holy Spirit and is born instead of imposed by a mechanism. Do we bear one another's burdens? Are we really able as a good friend to listen to confessions without curiosity and without talking about them to others? Are we able to minister to each other in this manner as Christ ministered to us? Even Luther, who stressed so much the priesthood of all believers, said that every Christian should be able to be a Christ to his brother.

The difference between the Christian fellowship and the ministry of the Christian in the world is found in the fact that within the fellowship there is a mutual response and forgiveness which is not only offered but also accepted and lived.[74] The Christian fellowship is marked, not merely by a forgiving attitude, but also by accepting forgivenness; not by just giving aid, but also by receiving aid graciously, as all of us were helped and forgiven before we could help and forgive. In other words, here reconciliation is not merely proclaimed and promised; it has become a completed act. That is what it means to belong to the Body of Christ. Perhaps evangelism should start within and do some housecleaning before preaching to the outside world.

Thus, Bonhoeffer's objection to spirituality does not mean that he denies the work of the Spirit of God. On the contrary, by pointing out the confusing usage of the word, he wants to clear our minds for the real meaning of the word "spiritual" in the sense of sharing in the Spirit of Christ which sheds abroad into human hearts the love that is not jealous or boastful, not arrogant or rude, which bears all things, believes all things, hopes all things, endures all things.

This love meets people through human channels. These human channels do not need to be spiritual people in the sense of cultured individuals. Rather, they need to be spiritual in the sense of being born of the Spirit of God who uses their lives of flesh and blood to rouse in Twentieth-Century irreligious man a sense of the "above" and the "beyond." But, in doing this, it never concedes that they are apart from the world which God made, loved, and redeemed.

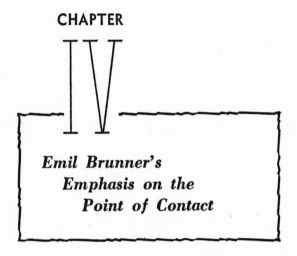

Emil Brunner's
Emphasis on the
Point of Contact

MAN REMAINS RESPONSIBLE

4

MAN REMAINS RESPONSIBLE

Emil Brunner's Emphasis on the Point
of Contact

SENSE OR NONSENSE?

*I*n a discussion between a Christian and an agnostic there occurred that kind of interesting moment which all of us who have engaged in the Christian witness have experienced in some way or other. The misconceptions of the Christian faith had been cleared away. The agnostic had admitted that he had accused Christianity in general of dishonesty and that, in the course of the conversation, it had dawned upon him that this could not be said of all its forms. Upon being asked whether the things which had been said about Christ and God made sense to him, he replied: "They make sense all right, but they do not live for me."

The agnostic was a follower of the philosophical school of linguistic analysis; but he was not one who denied that statements of faith, transcending sense experience, could be meaningful. Rather, he was of the opinion that, for some people, these things "lived" —but how and why, he could not explain. Apparently, something else was needed to be a Christian even if one had grown up in an environment where the Christian faith had been discussed and lived by committed people.

An example like this illustrates two factors which all of us have to face in the communication of the gospel: our responsibility to be clear and comprehensible and God's initiative in making our witness come to life.

OUR WITNESS NEEDS TO BE CLEAR

We are told that one Sunday Martin Luther went into the pulpit without sufficient preparation. He was not ready to give his message; and, remembering the promise that the Holy Spirit would guide all preachers, he decided to rely on Him and let Him do the preparatory work. When Luther preached his sermon, the Holy Spirit gave His witness indeed. He whispered all the time: "Martin, you have been lazy."

The task of theology, according to Emil Brunner, is to present the message of the church in clear and understandable terms before people of one's day and age. Every minister must know his field, and every lay witness must be acquainted with the content of his faith. He must be able to distinguish in his evangelistic task between what belongs to the Christian faith and what is a distortion of it.

The first reason that theology came into existence in the church was the need to protect the Christian faith from all sorts of wrong interpretations.[75] The second reason was the need for the adequate instruction of those who became members of the church and were going to be baptized. Theology grew out of the symbols or creeds taught in preparation for baptism. The third reason was the effort to give a short account of the message of the Bible, on the one hand based on scripture and on the other hand intended to enable the members of the church to read the Bible with more intelligence.

There are not only difficult passages in the Bible, but also many difficult themes and expressions which occur frequently. Unless the church gives instruction about the meaning of these, the Bible will remain a closed book in the lives of her members.

Although the Christian faith is not simply a matter of the mind, it certainly has something to do with our reason.[76] It is the task of theology to think clearly on the basis of God's revelation in the hope that our minds will be bound to Christ in obedience. Theology, therefore, is a second stage in our Christian life. It is distinguished from the life of worship and prayer in that it does not address God in the second person. In theology we speak about Him with the help of abstract thought. In the act of worship we address Him: "Our Father, who art in heaven. . . ." In theology we ask ourselves: "What does it mean when I call God 'Our Father'?"

God has given man intelligence, and the person who wants to be a Christian witness must use it. His witness must be clear and comprehensible. It must make "sense" from a preliminary point of view in that it hangs together and is capable of explanation.

OUR WITNESS MUST "RING A BELL"

Clarity and coherence, however, are not sufficient. It is man's responsibility to be able to give an account of his faith. All theology, according to Brunner, is missionary theology in the sense that its indirect task is to explain the faith to non-believers.[77] In I Peter 3:15 we read:

> Always be prepared to make a defense to anyone who calls you to account for the hope that is in you, yet do it with gentleness and reverence.

Man is used by God in the communication of the faith; but God, the Holy Spirit Himself, is the final agent in communication. It is up to Him whether we will click with our partner in conversation and whether our witness will ring a bell or not.

Rational thought, according to Brunner, does not lead to the knowledge of the only true God. All we can find out by mere argument is that there may be "something," but God is not "something." The God of reason is an object, but the God of Christian faith is subject. He is not the end of an argument, but reveals Himself through the word of the prophets and through Christ, the Word of God, in a personal encounter.

The knowledge of God, therefore, is not objective knowledge. It is personal contact. The word "to know" in the Bible—in the Old

Testament in particular—implies fellowship. "To know God" means to have encountered Him; and, in the encounter, He takes the initiative and acts as the Person who makes us truly persons.

This personal God, according to Brunner, is a great stumbling block to reason. Nobody of himself wants to give in to Pascal's word: "Not the God of the philosophers but the God of Abraham, Isaac and Jacob."

> In reason man remains by himself, shut up within the self-sufficient reason; in faith, however, he is approached by the self-revealing "Thou" who addresses him from without.[78]

Faith is the result of revelation, and revelation is the dialogue between God and man. In faith the monologue of thinking has been broken through by the Other. This event gives our reason another direction. Theology, therefore, should be thinking about God in bondage to Christ.

With respect to the evangelistic witness, this implies that the man who is addressed by the Christian is able to listen and to understand to a certain extent what he is saying. It makes sense, but only God can bring it to life so that it "lives" for him and true community is born, both between the partners in conversation and between them and God.

This is precisely what happened on Pentecost when the Apostles preached the good news of the resurrection of Jesus. They were inspired by the Spirit of God and of Christ in their witness. The account emphasizes that their speech was inspired by God. At the same time, the audience was moved to faith by the same Spirit of God so that the Apostles' witness came to life. The story also suggests that it was a miracle of hearing. The Holy Spirit is the final agent in the communication of the Christian faith.

MAN IN THE IMAGE OF GOD

For Emil Brunner this particular situation in which man, on the one hand, is able to hear and to listen but, on the other hand, is not able to understand or to grasp the word of God without special assistance of the Holy Spirit rests upon the fact that man has been made in the Image of God and, at the same time, is a sinner in need of redemption.[79]

Brunner is concerned that in the history of Christian thought the true meaning of the doctrine of the Image of God was soon lost because of a wrong interpretation of Genesis 1:26, "Then God said, 'Let us make man after our image, after our likeness. . . .' " As early as the church father, Ireneus, a distinction was made between "image" and "likeness" in the sense that the "image" was left in man but the "likeness" lost. The other factor involved is that from the earliest times the text was explained as though it read: "God laid his image in man" instead of "God made man in his image." Such an interpretation closed the eyes of theologians in the future to the fact that the Bible, not only in Genesis 1, but throughout the Old Testament, considers the image as a relationship in which man stands with respect to God instead of a function inherent in man's nature.

The result is well known. The theology of the Middle Ages—and still today of the Roman Catholic Church—is that man retained his rational nature after the fall. This is called the "image of God in man." On the natural level his life has remained intact; but he has lost the supernatural gifts of grace, faith, and complete knowledge of God. He has been deprived of the "likeness of God" through the fall.

On the basis of this theology, it is claimed that one can come to a preliminary right knowledge of God which needs supplementation by grace. Natural theology must be completed by revealed theology. Man can argue about the existence of God and decide that a prime mover, a final cause, an ultimate purpose must exist; but revelation must give the information about the Trinity. Roman Catholic theology, therefore, is more positive in its evaluation of the arguments for the existence of God than Protestant theology is today. The reason is the fact that the fall, in Roman Catholic theology, is mainly regarded as a deprivation. What has been left has remained intact, but it is incomplete.

The Reformation objected to this picture of a two-story structure, a realm of nature and a realm of grace. Grace for the Reformers does not merely supplement nature but restores it. The "image of God" to the Reformers was the same as the "likeness." They saw that the text in Genesis could not serve as a basis for this distinction as it contains a Hebrew parallelism, a way of speech, in which the same concept is expressed with two different terms. Yet, they could not maintain that no good was left in fallen man. Therefore, they spoke of certain traces which had remained and made man capable of systems of social justice and obedience to civil law.

With both solutions Brunner is dissatisfied. He agrees with the Reformers that we cannot think of the image and the likeness as two different things. But he disagrees with them in that he feels they have not been consistent in their doctrine of "traces of the image." On the one hand, it says too much as it suggests that man is not corrupted in his core or totally affected by the fall. On the other hand, it says too little as it suggests that man has been completely cut off from God and lost all humanity. This, Brunner thinks, would be fatal to maintain as it leaves out man's responsibility toward God which he can never lose even if he has lost the awareness of it.

THE IMAGE AS RELATIONSHIP

The Reformers have fallen into the error of speaking about the image of God in quantitative instead of qualitative terms, according to Brunner. If we do this, we must begin to figure out what "part" of the image in man is left; but the Bible does not justify such an approach. Brunner, therefore, chooses to make a distinction between what is called the formal and the material image. The formal image is the relationship between man and his Maker. Man has been created by the word of God, and he cannot make this undone. God, in making man and breathing the breath of life into his nostrils, has placed him in a unique relationship to Himself which man cannot escape even if he tries. This is what distinguishes man from the beasts, which also live by the word of God but which are not standing in this relationship of responsibility that marks human nature.

On the other hand, the Bible—particularly in the New Testament—seems to understand by the image of God something more than a relationship. For instance, when Christ is called the image of God, something different is meant. Christ responded positively in the relationship toward God which he shared with all human beings. So do Christians who are "in Christ" and who have been transformed in and through him. The formal relationship has become filled in these instances with a positive obedience, the real purpose of the relationship; and Brunner calls this the "material image."

RESPONSIBILITY

The implications of Brunner's doctrine of the Image of God are that man cannot escape his responsibility. He may not know the true ground of this responsibility, namely the God who made him;

but he senses that he is responsible either to himself or to his fellow men. These are indirect indications of his basic responsibility to God.

An illustration of this can be found in the work of Albert Camus. Camus' work is marked by a struggle to find certain norms in spite of the fact that God has died.

In his book, The Rebel,[80] he asks the question as to why man as a rebel soon becomes a tyrant. Why do human revolts fail by persistently going too far? Modern man should come to terms with murder and suicide, and he must do so without taking God into account. Camus, in other words, is in search of values; and the source for these values he tries to find in man himself, as a humanist does. There is a sense of responsibility in this search even if it is a responsibility to the self. Here Brunner would discover an indirect sign pointing to man's responsibility to God.

For the evangelistic witness this theology implies that we approach everybody in the awareness that each person stands in responsibility to God. When we proclaim God to a non-believer, we are not introducing a completely new factor. God may be unknown in that person's life, but He has been there all the time without the person knowing it.

Man, according to Brunner, is being addressed by God all the time. Brunner denies the validity of a natural theology, but asserts the meaning of natural revelation.[81] The two are not the same. Natural theology is the work of man; natural revelation is the work of God. The expression "natural revelation" is an unfortunate one because the word nature is pagan in origin; and, by nature, modern man primarily understands a closed entity which works by itself according to its own laws of cause and effect. Therefore, Brunner prefers to speak of "original revelation."

This means that, originally, man could notice the word of God in the work of His hands. Through the fall this has become impossible, but man nevertheless remains responsible and is held guilty for the fact that he cannot hear God in the manner in which He addresses him through His creation and in history. Man gives the wrong answer to God in the form of idolatry:

> Ever since the creation of the world his invisible nature, namely, his eternal power and deity, has been clearly perceived in the things that have been made. So they are without excuse; for although they knew God they did not honor him or give thanks to him, but they became futile in their thinking and their senseless minds were darkened. (Romans 1:20, 21)

61

Objectively speaking, God reveals Himself to man through the work of His hands and in His actions in the world; but man is incapable, subjectively speaking, of accepting this revelation.

Pagan religions, on the basis of this view, are not mere dreams of man. They are distortions of the response which man is called to make to something which is objective but which he is incapable of grasping except as it is revealed to him through the special revelation in Christ.

God's revelation in Christ does not come to man as something entirely new. It may be new in his consciousness; but, actually, the Word who came to redeem is the Word through whom man was made. People who have come to accept the Christian faith after abandoning another religion always have stressed the complete break; and yet, at the same time, they have admitted that their eyes were opened because of the fact that God had not left Himself without witness (cf. Acts 14:17) in the past in their own lives and in the history of the world. By faith our eyes are also opened for God's revelation in creation. Calvin spoke of the glasses which God gives us in His special revelation through which we are made capable of reading the book of His revelation in creation.[82]

THE POINT OF CONTACT

Man is responsible because he has spirit. Brunner does not want to divorce the body from the spirit of man. Such separation would be a mark of the contradiction which is the result of the fall. The body, together with the spirit of man, has been set in a responsible relationship to God; but God approaches man through man's spirit. Throughout the Bible, Brunner thinks, the spirit of man is the receptacle of God's Spirit so that the two should never be confused.[83] He quotes Romans 8:16:

> When we cry, "Abba! Father!" it is the Spirit himself bearing witness with our spirit that we are children of God.

Self-transcendence belongs to human nature, and this gift is not lost in fallen man. The Bible, indeed, speaks of the spirit of man in terms of his ability to stand outside himself and his world. We remember Proverbs 20:27:

> The spirit of man is the lamp of the Lord searching all his innermost parts.

And it is as though we hear an echo of this teaching in I Corinthians 2:11:

> For what person knows a man's thoughts except the spirit of the man which is in him? So also no one comprehends the thoughts of God except the Spirit of God.

God is Spirit, and man has spirit. But the distinction is made in the New Testament between mind (nous) and spirit (pneuma) in such a manner that fallen man has spirit in the sense of mind, but only the new man has spirit in the sense of pneuma: the new personality which is the material image of God in Christ. It is good for this reason, according to Brunner, to make a sharp distinction between the spirit of man and the Spirit of God.

The human mind "is the vessel, but not the source of God's word." [84] This expresses more clearly than any other statement what Brunner means by "the point of contact." He does not mean to say that every man has potential faith slumbering in the depths of his soul and that this part of him merely needs to be resuscitated in order to grow and blossom. The point of contact for Brunner is a formal one, not a material one. Man who hears the witness of the Christian is capable of having some understanding of what he is saying even if, of himself, he is incapable of grasping it as the word of God. The Holy Spirit is the final agent in communication; but in His work He engages the whole man, both of the Christian witness and of the man who is being addressed.

A storm of controversy once arose around Brunner's and Barth's teaching on the issue of the point of contact.[85] Barth, as we shall see, accepts a point of contact only in the sense that God creates it in grace. For Brunner the point of contact is a product of God's first creation and is present in all people, not only in believers: "All that the God who deals with us in His word and by His Spirit apprehends in man, in order to give him the gift of faith. And again all that he thus apprehends is created by Him, by His Word and His Spirit." [86]

The debate between the two theologians was connected with that on natural revelation. For Barth there is no natural revelation, partly because he understands something different by revelation—as we shall see in the next chapter—partly because he feels that there is no revelation except in Christ.

This may sound like a rather abstract or theoretical discussion; but we should not forget that, during the last World War, this was a tremendously important issue in the German church-struggle.

Brunner and Barth, today, both agree that there is no natural theology. It became a compelling necessity for the church to speak out on this issue. This the confessing church did in her *Barmer Thesen*, a statement rejecting and challenging the teachings also found in the church in Germany that, on the basis of natural revelation, the German people could come to the conclusion that their race needed to be protected and their territory extended.

Wherever man believes that he can derive the meaning of his life from God's revelation in nature and history, without God's special revelation in Christ, he ends up with the glorification of his own vitality and self-centered desires. In view of this trend, the German church made the pronouncement that man cannot know the will of God except in Christ, who judges our loyalties of natural kinship and calls us to a new obedience in the Kingdom of God.

THE DIALOGUE

The merit of Brunner's view on a formal point of contact is that it emphasizes the necessity of the dialogue. The Christian witness who enters into discussion with the world is not merely giving a monologue. He can trust that, to some extent, he can be understood by his partner in conversation. He can appeal to his mind as he draws analogies from human experience. He can appeal to a sense of responsibility as he points to the human relationship in which we live.

Thus, when entering into conversation with representatives of other religions, he does not merely discard the expressions of religiosity because he sees in them the efforts on man's part to come to a response to God addressing mankind. Even if he finds an attitude which is almost hostile to religion, he can see in this an indirect witness to God being at work with him:

> The fact that man whether he believes it or not, necessarily forms the idea of the absolute, is a sign that even fallen man, in virtue of the fact that the Spirit of God still remains near him, even when he, man, has become alienated from God—is still related to God.[87]

THE LANGUAGE OF FAITH

Man's ability for speech sets him apart from the animals and is part of the formal image in which he is created. It implies reason and the ability to abstract. For instance, if we use the word "house," we make a general picture on the basis of a number of houses we have seen in our lifetime. This ability is presupposed in our Christian witness, and we appeal through it to our hearers. We try to illustrate the content of faith with the help of experiences we have in common. But these analogies are used in order to indicate a reality which transcends ordinary sense-experience. In our witness we always should remain true to life; but, at the same time, we are speaking about the ground above and beyond it.

There is a philosophical school in our Twentieth Century with which a Christian witness has to come to terms. It is called the school of linguistic analysis. While existentialism is a present-day expression of synthetic reason, linguistic analysis is the work of analytic reason.

The representatives of this approach do not particularly want to come to a picture of a meaningful whole of reality; they merely ask the question of meaning. Does what we say make sense? The school came into existence in Vienna around the turn of the century and has Wittgenstein as its father. Today the school has many adherents in Britain. In the early stages, no statement was considered passable unless it could be verified by sense-experience. Wittgenstein's rule was: "One must be silent about that of which one cannot speak."

In such a case the limits of language are the limits of the world of sense-experience. Gradually, however, some representatives of this trend of thought have come to the conclusion that there are various categories of speech in which man expresses himself. Beside the ordinary or plain language, there is the language of poetry in which images are used in order to express man's reactions to the world about him. And religious language makes use of symbols in order to express more than human feelings and reactions. It employs these pictures to indicate the truth about what transcends the world of sense-experience.

The interesting aspect of what the school of linguistic analysis has done in some of its representatives is this: A clear appreciation has been gained for what might be called the "religious situation" in which a certain phrase that may not at first be meaningful to a person actually comes to life and gains its full meaning.[88]

There are analogies of such situations in everyday life, for instance, in the language of love; but the Bible ascribes this to a factor which is beyond human control, namely, the work of the Holy Spirit, who is the decisive agent in the communication of the gospel. The reason for this is that the Bible, as we shall see in our final chapter, does not look upon the images of the language of faith as mere inventions of our imagination but as having their basis and origin in the divine reality itself.

For us the school of linguistic analysis, in doing this work, has pointed to the mystery of the communication of the Christian faith through the Holy Spirit. The Spirit alone can make our witness "ring a bell" in the mind of the other; and, in doing so, we experience a repetition of the event of Pentecost.

PAUL ON THE AREOPAGUS

From the beginning of the Christian Church the scriptural passage describing Paul preaching on the Areopagus in Athens has been used as an illustration of the right approach in evangelism and missions. A great deal, however, depends on how we interpret the passage. Should we emphasize the beginning of the story or the end?

There are those who understand it as an advice to all who engage in dialogue with the world to begin with people on their own level. Paul adapted himself to the intellectuals in Athens and began with an expression of appreciation of their religious and cultural interests. He referred to the altar for the unknown god, using it as a "point of contact." He presupposed that man is inescapably religious and always searching for God even if he cannot call God by name. At the same time, he quoted a thinker and then a poet, Aratus, who were both adherents of the Stoic school of philosophy, in order to establish the common ground. These thinkers had tried to explain that God is immanent in the world; and Paul wanted to stress that he, too, thought of God as at work in the world around and within human lives. Some exegetes stop here and find in the story a justification for a presentation of the gospel as continuous with man's religiosity and thought.

On the other hand, we find those who hardly pay any attention to the first verses. They consider these merely as an introduction in which Paul wants to gain their attention and admiration as a cultured man. What he really had to say, they claim, is contained in the verses which tell about the transcendence of God, the fact that He is not the product of human hands, and that this God had revealed Himself in the Resurrection of Jesus Christ whom He appointed as Ruler of this world. They stress the discontinuity in the argument and draw our attention to the mocking as a result of Paul's preaching. The gospel is not acceptable to the natural man. It is foolishness to the Greeks.

There are some who go so far as to say that Paul made a wrong approach on the Areopagus. He wanted to appear as one of the philosophers of his day and age, but this was disastrous. As an Apostle he could not conceal the crucial difference between the Christian faith and pagan thought. Therefore, his approach fell flat. He should not have pretended to be a philosopher and should have started right off with the difference. They claim that there is not another example in the Bible which represents Paul as arguing in such a manner. He, therefore, must have felt that he had been wrong and gave up the method. After all, the meager harvest did not encourage a repetition of the approach, they claim.

It seems to us that it cannot be denied that Paul used a point of contact—not in the sense that the Athenians were on the right track, but that he recognized they had been searching. This search seems to be more than an effort of man alone. It seems to be provoked by the presence of God whom they cannot recognize or come to know on their own. In this context Paul brings the good news of the Christ who does not simply fulfil their strivings, but who is in some way the answer to them even if he judges the idolatrous form which their response had taken.

From Brunner we must learn that, in our dialogue with the world, whether we talk with a religious or a so-called a-religious person, we shall have to take the other seriously in his effort to come to terms with the truth of God. We will have to present the Christ in such a manner that, on the one hand, he is the revelation of God who has made man and, on the other, he is the one who reveals the human heart as turned into itself and leading man astray in order that he may heal the contradiction and restore man to wholeness.

Karl Barth's
View of the Uniqueness
of the Christian Faith

RELIGION AND THE CHRISTIAN FAITH

CHAPTER

V

Karl Barth's
View of the Uniqueness
of the Christian Faith

RELIGION AND THE CHRISTIAN FAITH

5

RELIGION
AND THE CHRISTIAN FAITH

Karl Barth's View of the Uniqueness
of the Christian Faith

FAITH AS THE ABOLITION OF RELIGION

arl Barth is a theologian who, in stronger terms than anyone else, has emphasized the uniqueness of Christian faith as compared with the expressions of all other forms of human religion. For him, man's religiosity is a fact; but it has no significance as a positive contribution that man makes toward his faith. On the contrary so far as Barth is concerned, in all cases where God has revealed Himself man tries to take over with his religion to distort the reality of the revelation. For Barth, therefore, revelation is not merely the opposite of religiosity in other religions. It is also within the Jewish faith and within Christianity itself.[89]

71

Consider, says Barth, the story of Israel. God had chosen His people and made Himself known to them in a unique manner. But they could not maintain this revelation in pure form. Their religiosity caused them to distort it from the beginning, and the prophets always had to scorn them for this. As soon as they had received the law, they began to worship Jahveh in the form of a bull because their religious nature tempted them to do this. The story of the golden calf is not a story of a people who invented gods but rather of a people who wanted to combine the revelation of the one true God with the ways of religion and worship of the surrounding tribes.

The feast is called a festival of Jahveh (Exodus 32:5). Why did Amos and Jeremiah object so vigorously against the cult of Israel (Amos 4:4, 5:5, 25, Jeremiah 7:21)? They objected because, instead of a means of worship provided by God Himself, the cult had turned into a tool used for the bribing of Deity. Man tried to justify himself by it instead of considering it as a God-given means of atonement and worship (cf. Leviticus 17:11).

Certainly, Israel's rejection of the Christ shows that no form of religion in itself can ever be called the true religion. It was in religious zeal that they nailed Him to the Cross, using the ideas and laws which had been kept in honor by organized religion.

The picture of the New Testament Church is not much different, according to Barth. The Apostles were certainly not chosen because of their religiosity. In their religious zeal, they quarrel over who will be the greatest in the Kingdom. In a religious mood, Peter forbids Jesus to speak of his passion. Later, the big fisherman even denies him (Matthew 16:22; 26:69 ss.). The disciples fall asleep in Gethsemane, and they are completely confused when the drama of Jesus' life on earth ends with the Crucifixion.

Paul later has great trouble chanelling religious passion which expressed itself in speaking in tongues and other ecstatic phenomena in the Early Church (I Corinthians 14). He is definitely restrained about his own religious experiences (II Corinthians 12). In other words, revelation is not a matter of genius, as Kierkegaard used to say. It is often assumed that, because the Jews had a genius for religion, Christ had to be born a Jew. In such a case, however, we forget that the Jews rejected him and that, in them, the whole human race expelled him from the earth and all human religion crucified him.

Religion is one of the expressions of being human, Barth admits. But, since man as a whole belongs to the realm of "flesh," i.e., of the creation in rebellion against God, his religious inclinations also will be constantly turned against the only true God. As things stand, man's religious nature provides him with all sorts of efforts to justify himself instead of making him wait for God, who alone can justify the sinner.

Barth distinguishes four forms of man's religion:

In the first place, man forms himself a deity. Where man follows his religious inclinations, he sets up gods for himself; and these deities, as a rule, are made in his own image. They are personifications and representations of his own needs and desires; and usually they are self-centered. The result is the picture Paul describes in Romans 1.

In the second place, man tries of himself to fulfil the law. Just as there is a natural religion which leads man to idolatry, so there is a natural morality which induces man to think that he can reach perfection by obeying rules which have been set up by man. In doing so, he thinks that he has fulfilled the final norm. But he does not arrive at gratitude because he actually does it himself. This is the point of Romans 2.

In the third place, man can turn to mysticism. This happens when, at certain times, people are dissatisfied with the existing religion. What they have tried to find without, they now intend to find within. The word mystic contains the word "muein," which means to close the eyes and the mouth because what is found is discovered within and cannot be expressed in words to the outside world. Mystics are known for their seclusion and separation.

Actually, mysticism is a form of rebellion against existing expressions of religion. But it is a rather mature form of rebellion. The mystic feels that he stands above the outward practices of most people, but he does not condemn them. He knows by intuition, if not in fact, that he lives by the system of the dominant religion of his time and place even though he wants to make it more inward.

The fourth form of religion is atheism. Atheism is a juvenile reaction against an existing religion in that it is mainly negative. It is against the forms and expressions of the current religious systems. One could say, according to Barth, that mysticism and atheism are the results of relative crises in forms of human religion; but this is not the absolute crisis which occurs in any form of human religion when revelation takes place. There is only one absolute crisis in the world of human religion, and this happens when God breaks through with His Spirit and convinces man of the hopelessness and helplessness of his own futile efforts to become reconciled. Then faith replaces religion. It does not simply add something to man's religiosity. It is a totally new thing. God Himself comes and dwells in the human heart through His Spirit and enables a man to proclaim that Jesus is Lord in word and deed (I Corinthians 12:3).

Christian theology, according to Barth, has sold its birthright in a slow process over the last four hundred years by trying to fit faith and revelation into the world of religion in general. The great theologians of the Reformation, like John Calvin, undoubtedly spoke of a "seed of religion" which was found in the human heart of everyone; but they did not build their theology on it. They were well aware of the fact that this seed, if left to itself, could never come to fruition, but would lead man inevitably into idolatry. They built their theology on the Word of God as it was perceived through the inward testimony of the Holy Spirit. The Holy Spirit, in other words, is the author of faith, and not man's religiosity.[90]

This soon changed, Barth claims. It became more and more a practice to make the Christian religion acceptable by trying to fit it in with what was called "natural religion."

Natural religion was man's own faith without the special aid of God. So we see that most works of Christian doctrine began with a long section on natural theology: the knowledge of God to which man can come without special revelation and the knowledge even of sin which he can gain in that manner. Later on, when the world of human religions was opened up for man, the effort was made to fit the Christian religion into the pattern of all human religions. Revelation was not mentioned except at the end in certain cases.

What happened, says Barth, is that, from the Eighteenth Century on, Christian doctrine did not deal with the religion of revelation, but rather with the revelation of religion. What the world of religion in general "revealed" was considered more important than the revelation of God in Christ. Christianity became a particular among the general, called religion.

It cannot be denied, of course, that revelation as such is claimed in many religions. An honest examination by the science of comparative religion shows that revelation is the phenomenon through which cultic, mythical, and moral content are derived from ordinances of the godhead. But this does not mean that, for this reason, a Christian should deal with revelation in his own faith as a problem. Revelation can only be dealt with in a positive attitude, namely that of reception. In other words, we must be open and frank about the fact that we are building upon it and not pretend to derive the content of revelation from a general religiosity or morality.

A POINT OF CONTACT?

One could almost write about Karl Barth's theology the verse taken from Isaiah 65:1:

> I was ready to be sought by those who did not ask for me;
> I was ready to be found by those who did not seek me.

God is able to break through the hard shell of man's resistance at times when man would least expect it. If the gospel enters a human heart, it brings a strange message and reality different from what was there before. This makes man hesitant to admit the existence of a point of contact.

The discussion between Barth and Emil Brunner on the subject has quieted down. Part of the reason that the topic is no longer raised in the same vigorous manner is that there undoubtedly was a misunderstanding between the two with regard to the meaning of terms. Brunner, as we saw in our last chapter, did not mean to say that a beginning of the true faith is in man. The human spirit may be the vessel of the Word of God, but it is not the source.

Brunner thinks of the point of contact in a formal way. It is man's capacity for language and responsibility. That is all. Barth, in dealing with the relationship between the human spirit and the divine Spirit, definitely admits that the Spirit of God is what holds man's life together whether there is faith or not. In every moment of man's life something takes place through which it becomes possible for man to meet the divine person as person, if God wills.[91]

The difference between Brunner and Barth is that Barth considers an analysis of man's spiritual power as of not too much significance for theology. He regards this as belonging to the realm of philosophical anthropology and does not deny its validity as such.[92]

Here also lies the danger of quoting Barth and drawing conclusions which go farther than Barth himself ever went. There are followers of his who do not have the tremendous erudition and openness which Barth himself has and who, merely taking his theological conclusion, excuse themselves from further work in the way of discussion with secular thought. Barth himself is constantly engaged in discussion with the world, as many interesting sections in his *Dogmatics* reveal.

In refusing the existence of a point of contact, Barth is afraid that speaking about it would draw people's attention away from the Christ. He admits that fallen man is not an animal, but he wants to emphasize that spirituality as such is not a prerogative which makes people more ready to enter the Kingdom.

In this respect Barth has something to say to our world which has become largely a-spiritual. Coming to faith is something different from finding an answer to the questions born of our egotistic desire and needs. Man, in coming to faith, is like the Virgin Mary when she answered the message of God with the words: "Behold I am the handmaid of the Lord; let it be to me according to your word" (Luke 1:38). This is a totally different attitude from finding one's egotism satisfied and discovering a way in which we can also go to heaven after having the rest of our needs fulfilled.

There is, according to Barth, no intentional apologetics or eristics. Inevitably, all theology is a form of witness; but debate with non-believers is not its first goal and certainly not its basis. People in Japan have raised the question as to why, in their country, the influence of this theologian is so important as compared with that of Brunner, who called his theology missionary.[93] The answer can be sought either in forms of Buddhism, which are close to Protestantism —as we shall see later on in this chapter—or in the fact that man is attracted by a straightforward presentation of the gospel without feeling that he is being tricked.

Too often we try to adapt our message in such a manner that the non-believer cannot see where it is different. Because of this, some prominent thinkers of the Existentialist School have said that they were more drawn by the thought of Barth than by the thought of Tillich and Brunner simply because this was straight theology and not a theology which merely used philosophy in order to convert other people. There is nothing more revolting in an evangelistic approach than the use of philosophy merely to show one's acquaintance with the field or to win people to one's own point of view. The man in the pew feels the same way if the clergyman pretends to be at home in all sorts of fields instead of holding to his own and doing a good job there.

Barth does not deny that human needs and border situations, like feelings of guilt and despair or facing death, can be instrumental in bringing people to faith. But if this occurs, he emphasizes, it is never the situation which brings them to faith. Rather, it is God who uses the situation as a token of a deeper need.

This, it seems to me, is an exceedingly valuable point. Whether a person is willing to use the expression "point of contact" in this sense or not, he must be clear about the fact that it is always an indirect one.

A difficult situation in a person's life may lead him to look for help outside. The temptation in such situations is to present God as an easy way out or as a stop-gap when we have reached our limit. What we do in such a case is merely to make a place for religiosity at the border of that person's life, and we should not be surprised if we never see him again as soon as the emergency is past. We have given in to his desire to use God for his own ends. Faith on the other hand, is not man-centered as religion is. Faith is God-centered and requires sacrifice. It leaves the mystery, which is revealed to us, a mystery.

All of us know that difficult situations, in themselves, easily lead people to a fatal despair or to a pagan or stoic form of resignation or, perhaps, to rebellion. The Bible speaks of a sorrow unto the world which works death (II Corinthians 7:10). If it happens that our needs and the needs which the gospel presents as our deepest needs coincide, it is by the grace of God. Often God can make our relative need transparent to our deepest needs. This must be said if we look at the way Jesus talked with the publicans and the sinners. Their eyes were opened, and they saw that he was not merely the answer to their own trouble but that their trouble was a token of the basic need of the world. Their sin became an expression of the estrangement of the race, and he had come to heal it.

Thus, we may never accuse Barth of just throwing the gospel at people like a stone. What he wants to emphasize is that, even in the most troublesome set of circumstances—which to a believer is so clearly the result of man's deepest need—a person does not automatically come to faith even if we talk to him and try to make him see what we see. If he does, we have become the instruments of God who Himself opened the eyes of this person. Barth would say that these "points of contact" are created by God, but that they are not already present in the life of man.

REVELATION

Revelation in Barth is something different from the way in which theologians like Calvin and Brunner have understood it.[94] This is another cause for misunderstanding.

Barth denies the existence of natural theology. In this respect, he is not so different from most modern theologians. He also denies, however, natural or general revelation. In this respect he stands alone. Certainly, he deviates from the general tradition of Christian thought.

What does Barth mean by "revelation?" For Calvin, revelation is an act of God regardless of man's response. So it is for Brunner. God is at work and addressing man through the works of His creation and through history in general; but man, of himself, cannot hear or understand God. Calvin used the illustration of the glasses which we need in order to read and which are provided in the Holy Scriptures. Through them the book of God's creation becomes readable. Without this subjective work of the Holy Spirit within the heart of the individual, man is unable to hear and see. Barth is of the opinion that if the work of God in creation cannot be perceived by natural man, the term "revelation" should not be used for it. Revelation for him is the completed event in which God not only acts, objectively, outside, but also, subjectively, in the heart, by opening the eyes of man so that he sees and the ears so that he hears. Therefore he refuses to use the term "general revelation" because, in his opinion, revelation is always specific.

Here, again, one may differ from Barth but learn from the point he makes. Revelation in creation is, indeed, received only when a person stands in faith and thus looks back and around. From the point of view of faith, we can say that God did not leave Himself without witness in the pagan world and that He has not left Himself without witness in people's lives in the past. But this becomes a reality only in faith. Christ revealed the heart of God, but the people of his day walked past him unless the Spirit made them see. The Bible is called the Word of God, and the minister proclaims it from the pulpit; but only if the Spirit of God makes us understand can we speak of revelation in the full sense.

The Holy Spirit for Barth is God the Redeemer who sets man free so that he can see and understand. Without Him all our efforts to convert anybody are vain. The Spirit of God is the subjective agent of the event of revelation: God within man, but not as a part of man's constitution. Therefore, conversion is not a possibility of man but rests with God's initiative.

THE CHURCH'S TEMPTATION

Spirituality in the sense of cultivation of man's spirit is not a particular asset with regard to faith within this frame of thought. It is a necessity and commandment, but it does not particularly predispose man for faith. "Blessed are the poor in spirit" is the warning which we hear in Barth's theology, as in Bonhoeffer's thought. In fact, Barth explains how the danger becomes acute if the church tries to be spiritual in the secular sense.

Barth distinguishes three phases in the life of the church in which the gospel was almost surrendered to man's power rather than to God's. First of all, there is the period of the early Christian Church until Constantine. The temptation to be proud of worldly achievement was not great. Paul, in I Corinthians 1:26-29, looking over his congregation, says:

> Not many of you were wise according to worldly standards, not many were powerful, not many were of noble birth; but God chose what is foolish in the world to shame the wise, God chose what is weak in the world to shame the strong, God chose what is low and despised in the world, even things that are not, to bring to nothing things that are, so that no human being might boast in the presence of God.

The early Christians felt themselves strangers and sojourners in this world, and they were not ashamed of it since they were conscious of being travellers to a better land (Hebrews 11). Being a Christian did not get one far in the realm of politics, art, and social life. They realized their weakness; and, in their weakness, they were strong— strong by the Spirit of God, and not by their own spirit. They knew what the first beatitude meant.

On the other hand, the church can never live in isolation. Some of its leaders realized how a pagan culture was in decay, and they grasped this as an opportunity to make Christianity acceptable to the world. Many people were spiritually rootless in an age of transition. It was very tempting for them to present the Christian faith as the kind of religion which was called and destined to preserve the best spiritual achievements of the culture which was about to perish.

The apologists took this line of approach. The strange element of the gospel was smoothed a bit. Tertullian and others protested by claiming that the gospel and the world of culture could not be reconciled. The result of this development was that the emphasis on spiritual poverty and the power of revelation yielded to the rise of syncretism. The church had become aware of her strength, but it was not always the strength of God.

The second stage in the history of the Christian Church in which a new idea of strength became current is found in the church of the Middle Ages: the *Corpus Christianum* idea. When Constantine had made Christianity acceptable, and it gradually became an asset to gain position and influence, spiritual superiority became intellectual superiority; and political power was combined with the gospel. The result was ambiguous. The real idea of strength-in-weakness gradually disappeared. The church backed the crusades and was involved in the investiture conflicts. Holy wars were fought. Jews and pagans (like Moslems) who came into contact with the church in the Middle Ages did not really encounter a power which was different from their own. It was worldly through and through in spite of the prophetic protest of some minority groups and individuals. Christianity became the combination of the gospel and the particular expression—intellectual, moral, aesthetic—of certain nationalities. Particular national Christianities arose in which the church co-operated with the worldly authorities.

The third phase is that of the Renaissance in which Western man came of age and threw off the yoke of the church which he no longer needed. Man dared to stand on his own feet in the undertakings of science, politics, and art. He threw off domination by the church which, for a while, tried to prevent this growing independence.

The church today gives in to her fears and inferiority feelings by trying to make Christianity presentable to modern, independent man and by acting as though he can use faith to reach his goals. In reality, the church is pushed back into the position of a minority group as it was during the decline of the Roman Empire.

Missionary enterprises followed the trends of their days and presented national Christianities or ways of life to the pagan world. They have called forth, naturally, the reaction of African and Asiatic Churches which are following the lead. These tend to take over the idea of strength by coalition with worldly power or independent man rather than the idea of strength through weakness. The truth that Christianity cannot be identified with a way of life, a culture, a race, a nationality is only gradually dawning. The only solution is that the church learns from its predicament that it is thrown back upon its original attitude: "by grace alone."

Barth's protest is directed against all who use the name "Christian" too easily and identify cultures and ways of life, which indeed may have been partially influenced by the gospel, with the Christ in an unparadoxical manner. Missionary work and Christianity at large are suffering from the consequences of this attitude. In our evangelistic approach we must admit that Christ has been recrucified by Christianity over and over again and that there is no evangelism without admitting that the gospel has been and is still being carried in earthen vessels.

IS CHRISTIANITY SUPERIOR?

We may see all around us a decreasing religiosity. Christian churches over the world complain that inwardness seems to have disappeared. Bonhoeffer spoke of the era of complete lack of religion. Yet, at the same time, we see an increasing interest in forms of mysticism, particularly as they are imported from the Far East.

The person who is engaged in evangelism can no longer fulfil his task without having some idea of the relationship between Christianity and other religions. Our world has become one in the sense that life is shared through modern means of communication, and non-Christian religions recently have shown a certain missionary zeal. A good Moslem considers himself an ambassador of Allah. The Buddhists have launched a world mission. What do Christians have to say?

Commonly offered solutions are often the kind which do not recognize the uniqueness of the Christian faith because they merely compare Christianity with other religions on the basis of the same human inclination. One common answer is the following: "All religions are like different paths leading to the top of the mountain.

We may follow different routes—in the long run we will end up at the same peak." This answer is an expression of syncretism and looks upon religion as man's urge to seek the divine, an urge which he can successfully follow.

A second type of solution is rather intellectualistic and claims that Christianity is "superior" to other religions. The other religions, according to this view, are not entirely wrong. Rather, they are, in some way, stages on the road to God; but they do not arrive at the only true God. It is as with the different rungs of a ladder. There are religions of a lower type, like the animistic ones, and religions of a higher kind, like the spiritual ones. But none of them can be compared with the highest rung, which is Christianity. Christianity, it is claimed, is the crown upon all other religions.

Barth is concerned about these answers because they make no difference between the Christ and the Christian religion. *Christianity qua religion*, he says, is no better than any other religious system. It falls under the judgment of God, as the Bible shows us (cf. I Peter 4:17).

Not Christianity, but Christ, is unique; and he judges all human religion. This implies that we do not bring Christianity in evangelism, but Christ. We must point away from ourselves to him whom we bring.

The trouble with the first answer is that it is vague mysticism and indifferent to the question of truth. The trouble with the second answer is that Christianity is still considered superior. This, in reality, means that we say to the person whom we want to convince of our faith: You possess a little of the truth, I have more. On this basis, it is likely to remain in discussion on the level of human achievement. Christianity is considered mainly from the point of view of genius rather than of revelation, and Christians can pat themselves on the back that they are are a shade better than the rest.

Barth is of the opinion that nothing which we often claim to be unique in our religion is unique in the absolute sense, except Christ himself. Even the claim that Protestant Christianity is unique as a religion of grace cannot be validated. He quotes from the realm of comparative religion two instances which show that grace is known in human religion, to some extent, also outside Christianity.

The first instance is the Indian Bhakti religion. Bhakti means surrender. Within this religion, there is a group of believers who adhere to the cat-rule and a group which hold the monkey-rule. According to the cat-rule, the deity leads his people to salvation in such a way that he does everything, just as the mother-cat holds her kittens by the neck and carries them around without their being able to do anything. These can be compared with extreme Protestants. According to the monkey-rule, the diety saves people in such a manner that they cooperate, just as the young monkey is carried by the mother while he holds on to her. These can be compared with Pelagians and semi-Pelagians.

Another illustration, perhaps even clearer, is taken from a form of Buddhism. Zen Buddhism is a religion in which man is required to redeem himself through works and contemplation. The Jodo-Shin sect, however, stresses faith as a condition for salvation into the pure land which is a fore-portal to Nirvana. Genku, the representative of this sect, said: "Even sinners will enter life; how much more the righteous!" Shinran, founder of the Jodo-Shin Shu sect, went one step further and rejected all meritorious work: "If even good ones are able to enter, how much more will sinners!" For him, faith in the promise is a gift of diety.

Barth recognizes very important differences between these forms of religion and the Christian faith. Nevertheless, he drives home his point that even Protestant Christianity has parallels in the history of religion. It is remarkable how congregations of this sect in Japan have refused state support and become completely independent.

When Francis Xavier, the Roman missionary, came to Japan in 1549, he wrote home that he had detected the Lutheran heresy in Japan. Barth's own influence in Japan may be partly due to the similarity of structure between the Protestant religion and these forms of Buddhism.

For Barth, there is no true religion in the final sense except as a promise, just as there is not a righteous sinner except in promise. One can debate whether Barth has done enough justice to the work of the Holy Spirit in the Christian Church which was promised by Christ and would lead the church in all truth. He has a valuable point, however, in that the effort to call the Christian religion superior in itself is not correct and can only lead to gross misunderstanding.

Missionary work and evangelism are efforts under God to share with others who have not "heard" of Christ the things God has shown to us in His revelation by grace. Here is no chance for superiority. Grace is decisive, and grace is God's good will and favor.

All of us rebel against this act of God's revelation. In faith, we know that, even in our best religious moods, we oppose God's self-revelation. The story of faith and religion is the story of Jacob struggling with God at the Jabbok (Genesis 32:22-32). Man, in his religious inclination, fights God and seeks to know Him at the same time. God, in making Himself known, remains a mystery to man and weakens man. Jacob's thigh was touched, and he went through life limping.

God's strength is only performed in weakness. Paul knew that, when he was weak, he was strong (II Corinthians 12:10). This is true of all Christian witness. The result of God revealing Himself is that both exclaim: "I have seen God face to face and yet my life is preserved" (Genesis 32:30).

THE IMPORTANCE OF BARTH'S EMPHASIS

It is hard to predict whether man has reached the end of his religious resources, as Bonhoeffer thought. Barth himself does not deny the possibility that he will find new ways of expressing his efforts to reach the divine by his own effort. The story of man's religion is like the story of the spider in the children's song:

Inky pinky spider
went up the water spout.
Down came the rain . . .
and washed the spider out.
Out came the sun . . .
and dried up all the rain,
and inky pinky spider
went up the spout again. . .

It seems that man never tires of new efforts to satisfy his longing to "get there" himself. He may be disappointed in the results from time to time and change from one form of religion to another, but he somehow clings to the conviction that eventually he will reach his goal.

Whether a person is conscious of this situation or not, whether a man is outspokenly religious or at a stage in which he has given up striving, the message of the gospel is for him. All of us have encountered situations in which it was practically impossible to perceive any positive response even on the level of ordinary understanding. In these situations the words of the prophet offer our only hope:

I was ready to be sought by those who did not ask for me;
I was ready to be found by those who did not seek me. . . (Isaiah 65:1).

It is perhaps true that, in cases like these, where—rather unexpectedly—the light breaks through, something is shown to us of what basically takes place in the life of everyone who comes to faith: the creation of a new beginning, the birth from above.

CHAPTER

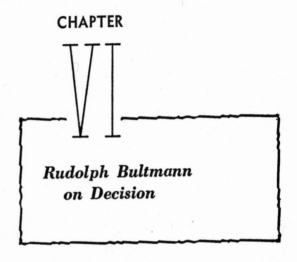

VI

Rudolph Bultmann on Decision

THE GOSPEL IN THE SPACE AGE

6

THE GOSPEL
IN THE SPACE AGE

Rudolf Bultmann on Decision

THE THREE-STORY UNIVERSE

*A*t one of his monthly sessions with the members of his Sunday school staff a minister was asked: "What do I say to one of my pupils who is wondering whether some day the astronauts might not bump into God?"

The question was not put in a manner which conveyed amusement. On the contrary, the teacher herself seemed a little upset by the child's remark and openly expressed her concern that space explorations were bothering her in her faith. She knew that God is not simply way up high; and yet the Bible is so full of sayings which indicate that He is in heaven that she honestly did not know

89

how to answer the child. She was bewildered: "If I maintain that God lives in heaven, they will question me further and ask if it will be possible to find Him some time in the future. If I say that, of course, heaven should not be understood literally, they will distrust me and not believe anything I have taught them over the years."

The confusion of this Sunday school teacher is typical of many people, both within the church and outside it, who have been left feeling uncertain as to what to think of those aspects of the biblical message which seem to bring us into conflict with the results of scientific discoveries. Many of our people seem to hold one type of thinking while in church on Sunday and another type during the days of the week. Are we to leave them in this dilemma?

When a minister, in his pastoral care, meets a person who is obviously mentally ill, he encourages that person to go to see a psychiatrist; but, on the Sunday following, he may preach on a text which tells of Jesus casting out the demons without making the slightest effort to connect the two.

Bultmann puts it in a blunt manner:

> It is impossible to use electric light and the wireless and to avail ourselves of modern medical and surgical discoveries, and at the same time to believe in the New Testament world of demons and spirits. We may think we can manage it in our own lives, but to expect others to do so is to make the Christian faith unintelligible and unacceptable to the modern world.[95]

A child had been told in Sunday school about heaven and hell. In the afternoon, when the sun had been shining on the front lawn of her home and she happened to go and sit down on it, she became frightened and ran to her mother telling her that hell was burning right underneath. She could feel it!

Many of us laugh at these experiences. Actually, they show how little prepared we are in the church to present the gospel in such a manner that it will stand up when children grow older and have to test these teachings in the world of everyday living and thinking. Why are we still surprised that so many become estranged from organized religion after they have left Sunday school?

We smile at the conflicts the church had with scientists when the Ptolemaic view that the earth is the center of the universe broke down. We think that it was rather naïve for her to take years before this change was discounted in her message. Actually, we are in a similar position today. On the way to work we talk to people about what the next step will be in space flight. On Sunday, however, we may hear that heaven is something man can never penetrate and about which we should not be too curious. The message is brought in terms which originate in an outdated picture of the world which Bultmann describes in the following manner:

> The world is viewed as a three-storied structure, with the earth in the centre, the heaven above, and the underworld beneath. Heaven is the abode of God and of celestial beings—the angels. The underworld is hell, the place of torment. Even the earth is more than the scene of natural, everyday events, of the trivial round and the common task. It is the scene of the supernatural activity of God and his angels on the one hand, and of Satan and his demons on the other.⁹⁶

Bultmann has asked the church a question which can no longer be evaded in the space age, namely, how we reconcile the mythological world view of the New Testament with our contemporary scientific outlook? Whatever we may think of the answer he proposes, we must join him in asking the question.

DEMYTHOLOGIZING THE NEW TESTAMENT

It is a pity that, on Ascension Thursday, most ministers do not have to preach. Very few have the courage to use the Sunday following for a sermon on the topic since it seems too difficult for them to explain the meaning of this aspect of the biblical message. If they forced themselves to tackle the problem, many would be more in favor of trying to give an answer to Bultmann's question.

The few who try it soon find out that the literal meaning is untenable in this day and age. They "demythologize," i.e., they interpret to their congregations the meaning of this part of the New Testament message.

On the one hand, they explain that the terms in which it is set forth are derived from a worldview which is not our own. On the other, they make clear that, precisely in those mythological terms, the element of exaltation and glorification is expressed—something which has great and profound significance for our faith in the Twentieth Century. In other words, they interpret Christ's Ascension symbolically and explain the imagery used. This is what "demythologizing" means.

More or less the same is done on other Sundays of the Christian year, but it is easier on those occasions to be vague about it; and the attitude of most ministers is based on a fear of disturbing their congregations with questions which might cause any form of doubt. But this attitude should belong to the past, according to Bultmann.

> At this point absolute clarity and ruthless honesty are essential for the academic theologian and for the parish priest. It is a duty they owe to themselves, to the Church they serve, and to those whom they seek to win for the Church. They must make it quite clear what their hearers are expected to accept and what they are not. At all costs the preacher must not leave his people in the dark about what he secretly eliminates, nor must he be in the dark about it himself.[97]

Bultmann is concerned about the evangelistic witness of the church. Are we presenting the gospel in such a manner that the people whom we confront with it have a chance to react to the message itself? Or do we make this impossible by putting up all sorts of barriers which are not really part of the message we must try to get across?

DO WE PUT THE SCANDAL IN THE RIGHT PLACE?

If, in our evangelistic enterprise, we act as though a non-Christian is asked to accept along with the Christ a worldview which has become outdated, we are guilty of putting the offense of the gospel in the wrong place.

Paul, in I Corinthians, spoke of the scandal of the Cross, meaning that everyone, before he comes to faith, is offended by the character of the message which humbles the proud and the wise. It is an offense to the Jews, with their moral conscience, that God accepts the sinner as he is. It is an offense to the Greek, who expects words of worldly wisdom but is confronted with the life of a carpenter. It is a scandal to the natural man in all of us that God comes as power in weakness. In this respect the gospel will always remain offensive to everybody.

But this is something totally different from a man-made obstacle that we put in the way of people's coming to faith. Often the church and many a Christian witness act as though the non-Christian world were offended by the gospel and that, for this reason, nothing more could be done about it. The plain truth is that the world is not offended at the Cross but at the wrong representation of the Christian faith which requires a sacrifice of intellect where no sacrifice is necessary. Our first responsibility as Christians is to give a responsible picture of the content of our faith.

SYMBOLIC LANGUAGE NECESSARY

> Myth speaks of the power or the powers which man supposes he experiences as the ground and limit of his world and of his own activity and suffering. He describes these powers in terms derived from the visible world, with its tangible objects and forces, and from human life, with its feelings, motives and potentialities.[98]

I know someone who, if he attends a liturgical church service in which he is asked to repeat the Apostles' Creed, is quite bothered by the content of this symbol. When the congregation arrives at the phrases, "born of the virgin Mary" and "he descended into hell," he keeps his mouth shut because he feels that it is not honest for a person in the Twentieth Century to say these things.

Twentieth-Century man has lost the feeling for imagery because he lives in a scientific and technological age in which he employs plain or exact language most of the time; and, unless he has learned to appreciate poetry, he has great trouble in understanding the imagery of the Bible. Dorothy Sayers reproaches modern man for his laziness in trying to understand Christian symbols.

> Why do you complain that the proposition that God is three-in-one is obscure and mystical and yet acquiesce meekly in the physicist's fundamental formula, "2P-PQ equals IH over 2Pi where I equals the square root of minus 1," when you know quite well that the square root of minus 1 is paradoxical and Pi is incalculable? [99]

We seem to have forgotten that the ancient creeds are "symbols" and need to be understood and read as such. The same is true of all language of faith.

In our preaching and witnessing we do not use exact language. We speak symbolically. A great deal of confusion in the evangelistic enterprise could be avoided if this were clear in the minds of all. We express the central concepts of the Christian faith in terms derived from human experience while, at the same time, we know that they transcend human experience. All our talk about God is a way of stammering, as Augustine said long ago. We must speak in order not to be completely silent. But no adequate words can be found.

This does not mean that we should slip into a mystical silence as though nothing could ever be said about the truths of faith. It rather requires that we have an idea of what we are doing in giving a Christian witness. The trouble is that a great many people engaged in evangelism leave the impression that they have no awareness of this. They talk about God as though they master Him as an object. All reverence and mystery are lacking, and the listener is left with a wrong impression of the Christian gospel.

The head of one of the Evangelical Academies in Germany once said that a large number of non-Christians come to the conferences in which the implications of the Christian faith for specific problems of social and political life are discussed. All participants are invited to attend a short service at the beginning of the day. Usually, the language of the hymns causes these non-Christians the greatest trouble. They tell about this when they are asked if the service has been meaningful to them. They have difficulty in grasping the meaning of the symbolic language used in the hymns of the church because, in their whole life, they have been accustomed to a different kind of language. Take, for example, this well-known hymn:

> Angels, help us to adore Him;
> Ye behold Him face to face;
> Sun and moon, bow down before Him;
> Dwellers all in time and space.

We can be certain that a great many churchgoers today face a similar problem. The difference is that so many of them do not even bother to ask for the meaning. They sing their hymns mechanically as they have sung them from their childhood. The sounds are familiar. For them the best medicine may be to worship some time in a church where another language is spoken or to try to read the Bible in another tongue. It is astonishing how figurative then the language appears or how absolutely meaningless it becomes unless it is taken symbolically.

MAN IN DECISION

It is Bultmann's advice that the mythological language of the New Testament should not be interpreted cosmologically, but rather existentially.[100] He is an admirer of the existentialist philosopher Heidegger, who has built his thought around the concept of man's self-understanding; [101] and Bultmann thinks that this is a fit tool for the reinterpretation of the gospel in the Twentieth Century.

Man is always man in decision. The gospel should not be brought in mythological terms, nor in objective scientific words, but rather in an existentialist framework in order to do justice to its meaning for us today.

94

We are not going to discuss here the question as to whether or not this is too narrow a basis for the interpretation of the gospel. The point is that Bultmann has laid his finger on a sore spot in the preaching of the church. The element of decision is often left out. We present a theological or philosophical truth and act as though it does not make any difference whether people accept it or not. This is bound to have its effect on our attitude toward the world outside.

We look somewhat surprised when D. T. Niles tells us that a Christian is not really a Christian unless he wants to share with his friends that which means most to him in his life. If the members of the Christian church began to live this, all would turn into witnesses for Christ. Or does he not really mean much to us, so that we have given up trying to share our convictions with others because we have none?

THE CHRISTIAN YEAR

The poverty of our faith is particularly clear on the main festivals of the Christian Year. Churches are usually filled on these occasions, but the preaching is at its worst. The witness of the laity is poorest on these occasions. This is due to the fact that we think of Christ in objective terms only without stressing the core of the Christian message that, in him, God really encounters man in such a manner that we must make up our minds.

Why is it that today we are in a situation which is almost worse than that in which the early Christian Church found itself during the mid-winter festival in the days of the Roman Empire? At that time the small group of Christians had the courage to proclaim, when the world celebrated the feast of the invincible sun, that Christ is the sun of righteousness and that the Light of the world was born a human child.

Today Christians have fallen back into the practices of a pagan culture to such an extent that it is hardly possible for their children to get to know the true meaning of the birth of Christ. Commercialization of the feast emphasizes gift-giving as an exchange which has nothing to do with the sacrificial gift of God in His Son. Churches try to put Christ back into Christmas; but many a church-goer comes home disappointed, wondering whether the Christian faith still has anything at all to say in our day and age.

Reinhold Niebuhr, in a witty piece of writing, recalls going to church on a Christmas Eve hoping that he would miss the sermon. The great facts of salvation, he says, are there to be adored rather than to be explained rationally.

> Dogma is rationally petrified poetry which destroys part of the truth "embodied in the tale" in the effort to put it into precise terms.[102]

Does this mean that we should give up the effort to explain the meaning of the central events of the Christian faith? [103] Definitely not! Man is man in decision when faced by the central facts of the faith. In his decision, however, he is not left to himself. He will be able to realize the existential significance of them only if the Holy Spirit, the Spirit of Christ himself, makes him a participant in them. Again, we are back at the need of a clearer doctrine of the Holy Spirit with respect to the witness of the church.

We want to consider the meaning of the Christian festivals in the light of the doctrine of the Holy Spirit. In doing so, we follow Bultmann's advice that the gospel should be preached in such a manner that man is called upon to decide. Unfortunately, Bultmann offers little help in gaining a deeper understanding of the work of the Holy Spirit; and, in the following, we shall go our own way.

This is partly due to Bultmann's wide definition of "myth" in which he applies the concept not only to the worldview in which the good news of the New Testament is expressed, but also to the content of the message. "Myth," for Bultmann, comprises all truth about the divine as it is expressed in terms derived from human experience. The New Testament, however, does not present the symbolic language about God as the mere product of man's imagination but, rather, as the result of the work of the Holy Spirit, who takes analogies from the work of His own creation.

In the Bible, human life is not divinized. Such kind of pagan myths are absolutely rejected.[104] The language used of God has its origin in the divine reality which is the ground and prototype of all human experience. Thus, when the Bible speaks of the Fatherhood of God, this is not the product of man's fanciful imagination, as Freud believed, but an indication of the reality which precedes and transcends human fatherhood.

> For this reason I bow my knees before the Father, from whom every family in heaven and on earth is named. . . . (Ephesians 3:14)

Our "stammering" the language of faith is not caused by a lack in God, but rather by the broken manner in which, alone, we are capable in this life of grasping the truths of faith. Nevertheless, in spite of our inadequacy, we must try to express these truths, trusting the guidance of the Spirit.

THE MEANING OF PENTECOST

Many of our churches make quite a fuss over the observance of the anniversary of their church building. A special speaker is invited. Suppers are held, and the memory of those who were connected with the erection of the edifice is celebrated.

Pentecost is the anniversary of the world wide church of Christ. Without the events that took place on the first Pentecost, the church would be a religious movement; but it would not be the church as the Body of Christ. The fact that we have neglected this festival is proof that we have forgotten what it means to be the Body of Christ and what it takes to be a Christian.

Being a Christian has become identified with being a member of a Christian civilization in which the majority join the church at a certain age because it is the thing to do. But Paul tells us that one cannot be a Christian unless he has Christ's Spirit within him (cf. Romans 8:9).

It is impossible to celebrate any of the Christian festivals except in the light of this one. Without Pentecost, the birth, life, death, and resurrection of Jesus would be memorable events in the life of a certain great personality who lived long ago; but they would have nothing to do with our personal lives except insofar as he might become a good example for us to imitate or admire.

Pentecost means that God who is for us—God, the Father, and who is God with us—God, the Son, is also God, who is willing to dwell within our hearts and give us new life—God, the Holy Spirit. The transcendent God, who is above and in all that He has created, applies in the human heart what Christ has done. The New Testament explains that the birth, the life, the death, and the resurrection of Jesus are realities before and apart from our participation in them. At the same time, it urges us to come to a decision about them. These are events in which God encounters us, even if they happened long ago. Through the Holy Spirit we may become participants in them.

97

Nothing new, therefore, is added to the central facts of salvation on the day of Pentecost. The difference is that now the great deeds of God come to life within human beings all over the world. No wonder that the World Council of Churches issues a message on Pentecost every year to remind the churches of the importance of the fact that, among all nations, people share in the new humanity of Jesus, which binds mankind together and is the only basis for the unity of the family of man. Logically speaking, Pentecost does not follow the other feasts of the Christian Year. It is presupposed in all of them if we celebrate them in the true manner as having significance for us in our own day and age.

CHRISTMAS

Christmas, by itself as the birthday of Jesus, could lend itself to a great deal of sentimentality, which is most welcome in winter time. It could even remind people of the new beginning which takes place in the birth of each child and strengthen them in their hope for the new year about to start. It may even be the feast of human good will; and, where this happens very easily, we may interpret generosity determined by selfish motives as continuous with the love of God.

In the light of Pentecost, however, we are not left to ourselves in our effort to cheer up a cold world torn apart by human strife and suspicion. The child Jesus, born in Bethlehem, grew up to be a man. He died and rose again. He has come back in the Spirit who was given on Pentecost:

> God, having raised up his servant, sent him to you first, to bless you in turning everyone of you from your wickedness. (Acts 3:26)

The Christ must be born in us. This is the decision before which Christmas places us. Not that we can cause this to happen to ourselves, but we are asked to make up our minds whether we will continue in our own spirit or in the Spirit of the Christ child.

The doctrine of the Virgin Birth, in the light of Pentecost, is certainly not a tool to prove the divinity of Christ in a biological manner. The doctrine has its antecedents in the Old Testament in the stories of the miraculous births of men like Isaac, Samson, and Samuel. The same meaning is found in the story of the birth of John the Baptist, who stands between the Testaments. In all these instances we are told that there were no children in those marriages and that, humanly speaking, it was impossible to have them. The miraculous births of these men of God point to the wondrous character of God's saving acts.

In the case of Jesus, God not only gave a Man who spoke the word of God but also one who was actually the Word of God taking on human nature. Thus, all expressions of human creativity are considered unimportant in the light of this event.[105]

The same is true of our birth from above. We must notice that John the Evangelist has his parallel to the story of the Virgin Birth in the twelfth and thirteenth verses of the well-known first chapter of his Gospel:

> But to all who received him, who believed in his name, he gave power to become children of God; who were born, not of blood nor of the will of the flesh nor of the will of man, but of God.

When a man comes to faith, all human creativity and religiosity seem nothing as compared with the new beginning, the new creation, which takes place. Man, in the act of faith, is like the Virgin Mary, who asked in wonder: "How can this be . . . ?" At the same time, he overcomes his doubt through surrender, as Mary did: "Behold, I am the handmaid of the Lord; let it be to me according to your word" (Luke 1:34, 38).

There is no Christmas without the surrender of our spirits to the Spirit of God, who alone is able to create a new beginning. There is no Christmas without Pentecost.

GOOD FRIDAY

Camus says of the death of Christ:

> Say, do you know why he was crucified . . . ?
> Well, there were heaps of reasons for that. . . .
> Did he really not know them? . . .
> The children of Judea massacred while his parents were taking him to a safe place—why did they die if not because of him? . . .
> . . . crime consists less in making others die than in not dying oneself! . . .
> He cried aloud his agony and that's why I love him, my friend. . . .
> The unfortunate thing is that he left us alone, to carry on, . . . knowing in turn what he knew but incapable of doing what he did and of dying like him. . . .[106]

These words interpret very well the feeling of many a churchgoer on Good Friday: "he left us alone to carry on . . . incapable of . . .

99

dying like him." It must be the feeling of all who look upon Christ's death as the end of a martyr, too noble and too good for this world.

But Christ is not like Socrates, who merely set an example for his pupils when, with a balanced mind, he drank the cup of poison in their presence. Jesus did not want to die. The scenes in Gethsemane and on Golgotha are not portrayals of a man who defied death but revelations of one who struggled with it.

The Christian Church celebrates Good Friday in the light of Pentecost. This implies that the call to discipleship becomes the call to watch with him in Gethsemane and to share in the sufferings of a world from which God seems to have disappeared. Nobody is capable of doing this on his own, nor do we want this of ourselves. But in the strength of the Spirit of God it can be done. Then, in the midst of desolation, the joy of Easter can be experienced because Good Friday, for a Christian, is never separated from Easter even as Easter is never without Good Friday.

There is a great deal of questioning among people both in and outside the church about the validity of doctrines of the atonement which stress that, because of the fate of one innocent person, others can go free. Expressions like "satisfaction" can so easily be presented in a manner suggesting that, on Good Friday, something of a contract took place between Christ and God. On the other hand, many also are dissatisfied with a presentation of the death of Christ as a moving story which should inspire man to abandon his selfish interests.

The solution to these questions does not lie in our denial of the "once for all" aspect of the life and death of Christ in its unique significance. On the contrary, without the objective meaning of Good Friday, Christ's sacrifice would have no meaning for us today.

Theo Preiss has spoken of a juridical mysticism in the biblical writings.[107] What he means by this expression is that, on the one hand, these events have an objective significance apart from and before our acceptance of them; but, on the other hand, they must become part of our lives. We must become incorporated into them. In Christ we must not only be born from above but also die to self in order to rise to a new life.

True disciples know what it is to be persecuted for his and for righteousness' sake. They do not hesitate to take their cross upon themselves. This is the decision before which Good Friday places us: Are we able to say with the Apostle that we are being poured out as a libation (Philippians 2:17)? For the Christian, there is no escape from Good Friday.

> Now, I rejoice in my suffering for your sake, and in my flesh I complete what is lacking in Christ's affliction for the sake of his body, that is the church. . . . (Colossians 1:24)

EASTER

At no time are our churches more filled and confused than on Easter. On the one hand, it is still considered the most important festival; and, on the other, people are at a complete loss as to what to think of it. As we saw in our first chapter, if they follow the idealist trend of thought, they are likely to see in the Easter event a confirmation of man's belief in the immortality of the soul. If they are naturalists, they reduce it to the joy over the cycle of nature in which life in springtime follows the death of fall and winter.

If, in contrast with these predominant modes of thought, we maintain the resurrection as something which can be "proved" by the empty tomb, we contradict even Matthew, the evangelist who knew that the empty tomb in itself could prove any number of things (cf. Matthew 28:13 ss.). The symbol of the empty tomb, like that of the Virgin Birth, does not "prove" a truth. These symbols only speak to us once we have come to faith in the incarnation and the resurrection.

Easter is something that took place both in the life of Jesus and in the life of the Apostles. It was the fulfillment of the life of Jesus in a manner which God alone could work, the consummation of his life lived in body and soul. The resurrection stories stammer about this in such a manner that they warn us not to think of it as merely spiritual nor as crudely material. The new creation became a reality, and the New Testament tells us that he is what we shall be.

Too often, however, the good news of the resurrection is preached as though it concerned merely our hereafter. In the light of Pentecost, it is something which begins for the Christian here and now.

For Paul, the unity of Good Friday and Easter in the life of a Christian is symbolized in holy baptism. Through the power of the Spirit a man dies to self and rises to a new life in dedication to God (Romans 6:5 ss.):

101

For if we have been united with him in a death like his, we shall certainly be united with him in a resurrection like his. We know that our old self was crucified with him so that the sinful body might be destroyed and we might no longer be enslaved to sin.

The resurrection, in other words, begins here and now in the form of down-to-earth obedience to God within the circumstances of everyday life. In contrast to our modern age, which is willing to listen to a message of Easter without the implications of Good Friday, the Bible presents the two experiences as inseparable:

> . . . that I may know him and the power of his resurrection, and may share in his sufferings, becoming like him in his death, that if possible I may attain the resurrection from the dead. (Philippians 3:10, 11)

Easter gives us the key to the life of obedience. Within the church itself there is a great deal of confusion as to what the right kind of life is. We live in a state of moral bewilderment in several areas. For many, Christianity means nothing more than the following of a traditional code. For others it is tied up with the life of Jesus, but in such a way that he set the example and we are basically left to ourselves to follow him and pull ourselves up by the bootstraps.

Easter places us before the decision. This is not a decision as to whether we will grit our teeth in trying to lead a perfect life. It is the decision as to whether we will find the resources for our new obedience in ourselves or in the Christ who rose from the dead and who will give us a part of his victory.

The time is past for the church to teach conventional rules for the sake of convention only. The confusion is actually twofold. In the first place, people are wondering: "What is the Christian life?" In the second place, they ask: "Where will we get the motivation to live it?" And both these questions are answered in the Christian message of Christ's resurrection. Paul says in the sixth chapter of Romans that a Christian does not lead the Christian life in order to be loved by God, but because he is loved by God. In Christ we have died to ourselves. This is a fact we must believe. The imperative of the Christian life is based on this fact, that in Christ we have overcome ourselves and risen to a life in fellowship with God. "So you must consider yourselves dead to sin and alive to God in Christ Jesus" (Romans 6:11).

Christian faith is something totally different from moralism—because of Easter. Any effort to reverse the order and pretend that a

Christian leads a good life in order to earn the grace of God is an absolute denial of Christ's resurrection. In the first place, we do not know what the good life is apart from Christ; and, in the second place, we cannot live it without the aid of his Spirit. "Be what you are," the Easter message tells us. Allow the Spirit of God to realize in your life what in Christ has become a perfect reality.

After we have seen that Easter has relevance for our daily lives in this world, we must also remember that the complete fulfillment of this new creation is something which awaits its consummation. There is a remarkable expression which is used of the Holy Spirit as He applies the work of Christ in human lives. He is called the "down payment" (II Corinthians 1:22, Ephesians 1:14) of the glory for which we may hope. In other words, Christians are people who always look forward. The writer of I John (3:2, 3) puts it in the following manner:

> Beloved, we are God's children now; it does not yet appear what we shall be, but we know that when he appears we shall be like him, for we shall see him as he is. And everyone who thus hopes in him purifies himself as he is pure.

ASCENSION

Ascension is the feast of pilgrims. One of the reasons that Ascension has lost its meaning for the church of today is that she has lost the awareness of "being on her way."

> Let not your heart be troubled; believe in God, believe also in me. In my Father's house are many rooms; if it were not so, would I have told you that I go to prepare a place for you? And when I go and prepare a place for you, I will come again and will take you to myself, that where I am you may be also. (John 14:1-3)

The familiar words from the fourteenth chapter of John speak in symbolic language of the true home of a Christian. A Christian is a citizen of the Kingdom of God. He obeys the laws of that realm first of all. Jesus is his King, and Ascension is the festival of his enthronement. The cloud which took him away from the Apostles' sight is a symbol of both his hiddenness and his glory.

If Jesus, then, is the King of the realm to which we owe primary allegiance, instead of staring ourselves blind on the outdated worldview in which this truth has been set in the New Testament, we should derive consolation from this message, particularly in an age when millions of people have no country they can call their own.

103

The Twentieth Century has been called the age of the displaced person. People have no roots. Even within continents and countries there is a mobility which is unprecedented. The church which is called to preach the message of the gospel to these people cannot do so unless she herself knows what it is to be "on the move." The church is the congregation of those who are on their way to a better land. The author of Hebrews 11 describes this as the essence of the faith. Ascension places us before the decision whether we are content with the *status quo* or are looking forward to the future.

Ascension, too, should be interpreted in the light of Pentecost. It has something to say for the Christian in his life here and now, and not only for the hereafter. In Colossians 3:1-3 this aspect of the Christian life has been expressed in the following manner:

> If then you have been raised with Christ, seek the things that are above, where Christ is, seated on the right hand of God. Set your mind on the things that are above, not on things that are on earth. For you have died, and your life is hid with Christ in God.

Christ is our true home. Our walk is in "heaven" (Philippians 3:20). This does not mean that Christians are "unworldly." On the contrary, right in the midst of this world, they live the life of obedience to the "heavenly" city.

Being a member of a church implies that we proclaim the rule of Christ over the whole of creation, also and particularly to those who live under Christ's rule without knowing it. As Cullmann has said, the church is the inner circle; and the world is the outside one. Both circles have the same center, namely Christ.[108] The church waits and works until both circles fall together. This will be when Christ is acknowledged as the King of all creation:

> . . . at the name of Jesus every knee should bow, in heaven and on earth and under the earth, and every tongue confess that Jesus Christ is Lord, to the glory of God the Father. (Philippians 2:10, 11)

Ascension is part of the victory of Christ. Therefore, we should not isolate it from his Cross and the resurrection. Actually, in the Gospel of John, Jesus is said to have been glorified in the Crucifixion (John 12:23) and to have been exalted or "lifted up" on the Cross (John 12:32). Similarly, a Christian may share in Christ's exaltation in the midst of his Cross-bearing through the work of the Holy Spirit who incorporates us into the risen and glorified Chirst. Here and now we begin to share in the new humanity of Jesus; and, as pilgrims, we look forward to the consummation of Christ's image in us.

> And we all, with unveiled face, beholding the glory of the Lord, are being changed into his likeness from one degree of glory to another; for this comes from the Lord who is the Spirit. (II Corinthians 5:18)

Such is the role of the Holy Spirit with regard to the Ascension. For ourselves, we can never forget that we are "stammering" when speaking about these things. The imagery of the Christian hope during our pilgrimage is most vividly expressed in the hymns of the church, and we must try to open people's eyes to their symbolism so that these hymns may have full meaning for them. Preaching and speaking about these matters is—and always will be—difficult but rewarding at the same time. We should not forget that a sermon is meant to lead to adoration; and, if it is not itself an act of thanksgiving, it is not worthy to be called proclamation of the gospel.

THE DECISION MADE FOR US

We have seen that the decision before which the life of Christ, as celebrated in the Christian festivals, places us is a peculiar one. It is not a choice which we can make of our own record. If we make the decision, we actually choose for him who has already chosen for us. We merely allow the Spirit of God to make the Christ a reality in our lives. God in Christ has decided in our favor. This is what the gospel proclaims. There is really only one choice left for us: to decide for him through the grace of God.

Conclusion

SUMMARY

Modern man is inclined to have a "nothing but" attitude with respect to his own nature. Idealists believe that man is nothing but a soul and forget that man is a creature. In the church, the approach has often been that man is nothing but a soul and that his body is a shell of negligible importance. Outside the church, moral standards are determined largely by the attitude that man is nothing but a body. Appreciation for man's spirit as his capacity for self-transcendence is almost nil.

Both attitudes, the idealist and the naturalist, are basically rationalistic. The Christian faith concerns the whole man, as Niebuhr has shown. He participates in the realms of nature and spirit and remains a creature in need of renewal in the core. Faith is not merely a rational decision, but a choice of man in his entirety, influenced by the Holy Spirit.

The philosophy which stresses man's involvement and man's living in decision on all levels of his life is called existentialism. Tillich calls existentialism the good luck of the Twentieth Century as it emphasizes a gap between what man essentially is and what he appears to be in existence. Thus, man cries out for redemption; and the church should be attentive wherever this quest for salvation is heard in the world of today in order to provide the answer from God's revelation. The dialectical relationship between the question asked by the world and the answer given in the church he calls the method of correlation.

Not all people, however, ask the question, Bonhoeffer says. There is an increasing lack of inwardness and religiosity today. This is so because man has come of age, and the church should not try to put Twentieth-Century man back into adolescence in order to make him ask for religion. We should not look upon man's extremity only as God's opportunity. God is not a stop-gap. He must be found in the center of life: in health as well as in sickness, in joy as well as in sorrow. Christians need to give a "worldly" interpretation of their faith before the world. This is given in the life of obedience and discipleship, which is participation in the death and resurrection of Jesus.

Our witness must be clear and stated in comprehensible terms. God has given man a mind with which he can think; and even if fallen man of himself is incapable of grasping the Christian witness as the Word of God, he can see that it makes sense. Therefore, Brunner maintains, we should enter into dialogue with the world. In approaching the non-Christian we want to make God a reality in his life: God, who made him and who has placed him in a unique relationship of responsibility. If the person responds, the Holy Spirit of God causes our witness to ring a bell in his life. The Holy Spirit is the final agent in the communication of the gospel. He is at work in both witness and listener when the response of faith is made.

When faith arises, says Barth, there is an absolutely new beginning, created by God. It is the birth from above. Faith in Christ, for this reason, is different from all forms of human religion, which is man's effort to reach the divine on his own. God is found by those who did not seek Him. Whether a person is religious or not does not matter in the final analysis: Faith is the absolute crisis in his life, whether he is a theist or an atheist. The church should not yield to the temptation of smoothing the strange and offensive character of the gospel. Faith means power in weakness, and the Twentieth-Century church is thrown back into the position of the early Christian Church which had to rely on grace alone.

"Do we really confront modern man with the Christ?" asks Rudolf Bultmann. Or do we put in his way all sorts of barriers which are man-made so that he does not have a chance to come to a decision?

The gospel admits that the Cross is a scandal or offense to the natural man. Do we put this scandal in the right place when we give our witness? We should be clear about what a non-Christian and a Christian are asked to accept in faith and what not.

Faith does not require a sacrifice of intellect in the sense that a person today must adhere to a three-story worldview as people did two thousand years ago. We must be aware of the fact that we speak in symbolic terms when we use religious language. Only if we take these factors into account can we put people before the real decision by making them face the Christ in whom God has made His decision in our favor.

THE KNOWLEDGE OF GOD AND THE KNOWLEDGE OF MAN

Evangelism requires the knowledge of God and the knowledge of man. Both go together. If we overemphasize the former, we do not do justice to the gospel in which God took upon Himself our human nature in Jesus Christ in order to make Himself known. God cannot be known in abstraction. God, in Himself, is no other than God as He meets us and speaks through human lives of flesh and blood, lived in obedience by the members of the Body of Christ.

Evangelism is never a merely spiritual affair. It is interpretation through word and deed. The gospel is taught and caught because, in Jesus, word and life were one. In our interpretation, however, we must be aware that we carry the treasure in earthen vessels.

On the other hand, if we think that the knowledge of man is sufficient, we may have profound insights into the human predicament but our religion will remain a method of self-improvement. Knowledge of man apart from the knowledge of God is a distortion. Such evangelism has no gospel to proclaim. It basically leaves man where he is even if it tries to provide him with a measure of self-understanding. Good evangelism always throws us back on the need for theology.

In the third place, we need to know the spiritual climate of our own day and age. How do people think of themselves? How do they live their everyday lives? Does God play a role in it? If so, is he the God of the Bible or some product of their wishful thinking who must help them out when the going gets tough? Do people ask the question of meaning in life, or have they given up living on a deeper level? Is modern man blind to symbols, and, if so, why? Is he content to feel like a piece of driftwood floating down the stream and doomed to disappear eventually in the maelstrom?

GOD'S GRACE AND HUMAN RESPONSIBILITY

Evangelism is a matter of God's grace. The Holy Spirit is the final agent in the communication of the Christian faith. Faith is a gift (Ephesians 2:8), and witness to the faith can be accomplished only in the spirit of utter dependence on God. Evangelism requires a doctrine of the Holy Spirit which makes clear that people who are confronted with the gospel are not left to themselves to imitate a mere example set by Christ. With the proclamation goes the promise of the Holy Spirit, who is the Spirit of Pentecost.

The event of Pentecost is repeated wherever a person responds to the Christian witness. The Holy Spirit is the subjective agent in the event of revelation, and He enables man to participate in the benefits of Christ. He alone works the positive decision in response to God's.

The decision of faith is made by man at the same time. This is not an event in which we can make a neat distinction as to what is done by God and what is done by man. We appeal to man's responsibility in placing him before the decision, but the paradox of faith must be maintained:

> Work out your own salvation in fear and trembling; for God is at work in you, both to will and to work for his good pleasure. (Philippians 2:12, 13)

The same is true of the Christian witness. Christians have the obligation to witness in word and deed. They must be clear and comprehensible in what they say, but the Holy Spirit alone can bring their witness to life and make it "click."

If either factor is neglected, we have a distortion of the method of evangelism. On the one hand, people who merely stress God's grace are likely to forget that the Holy Spirit begins where man is. Evangelism implies entering into the lives of other people in the spirit of compassion, standing where they stand in solidarity with them and asking the question with—and sometimes for—them.

Evangelism requires that reconciliation be expressed within the life of the Christian fellowship and toward the outsider. The church must learn again to accept the unacceptable instead of being a social club of like-minded individuals with the same spiritual or moral ideals. Reconciliation flows through human channels.

Those who merely stress man's responsibility, on the other hand, are likely to stare themselves blind on a technique or the improvement of methods without changing or learning themselves. The curse of our churches in this age of the organization man is that we leave the impression that we can measure spiritual results with statistics and improve them by gadgets. Perfection of techniques merely means adding to the burden of chores if we do not try to take away the impediments which stand in people's way of coming to faith.

THE CRISIS IN EVANGELISM

The fact that our churches are fuller than ever, particularly on the great festivals of the Christian Year, should not close our eyes to the need of evangelism without and within the church. Church attendance is not enough. Increasing numbers of people are sincerely concerned about the content of the message and wonder whether Christianity has anything to offer at all. They are learning how to stand on their own feet and refuse to use religion as a necessary adornment of life at birth, marriage, and death. They are right in their protest against the confusion of religiosity with faith.

In view of this situation two things have become clear. The first is the fact that the methods to get people back to the faith have often been based on fear. We have tried to appeal to borderline situations mainly; and the result has been that, perhaps for a while, they became interested. But they soon came to believe that they could manage on their own again. There is no use putting an adolescent back into childhood. Religion as man's attempt to protect himself and to help himself morally has—fortunately—become outdated.

The second fact is this: The church has learned, in the light of this development, that within her own borders there is still a great deal which is supposed to rest on faith but which is actually motivated by human religion. The church can learn a great deal from the dialogue with the world. We have become aware that our usual approach, "Why don't you come to church with us?" has its hazards. What are they going to see in church? We have to do some housecleaning ourselves first. Do we live the life of reconciliation and mutual acceptance? Does the love of God shine through our attitudes and lives?

In other words, evangelism is not merely proselytizing or pressing other people into our mold. We learn from them at the same time. We approach them as persons.

Evangelism requires a theology, and all theology should be evangelism in some way. Sharing one's faith does not mean adding another organization to people's already over-burdened lives, but asking them to open their eyes to God, who is with them even in the places where they would least expect Him. It is the longing to share the outgoing love of God which alone can make life full and give it roots in an age of rootlessness. It aims at true community.

Evangelism demands a renewal of the church. We must become what we are: the Body of Christ or the fellowship of reconciliation. Instead of adding respectable people to the list of contributors, we must show the world what it means to accept people as they are.

Evangelism means learning how to live the life of discipleship and obedience in such a manner that others catch the spirit of gratitude in our lives and join in our response to God's decision for us in Jesus Christ our Lord.

Notes

1. "Antwort: Karl Barth zum siebzigsten Geburtstag am 10." Mai 1956, Zürich, 1956, p. 895.
2. Reinhold Niebuhr, "The Nature and Destiny of Man," Vols. I and II, London, 1945.
3. It cannot be denied that here and there the Greek terminology of Hellenistic thought has been taken over, as e.g. in Matthew 10:28 and II Corinthians 5:6-8, but such utterances do not change the basic point of view which does not split man but considers him as a whole. Cf. J. A. T. Robinson, "The Body," London, 1953.
4. D. T. Niles, "Preaching the Gospel of the Resurrection," Philadelphia, p. 21.
5. Cf. Article "Pneuma" in G. F. Kittel, "Theologisches Woerterbuch zum Neuen Testament," Band VI, pp. 330 ss.
6. R. Niebuhr, op. cit., Vol. I, p. 34.
7. Ibid., p. 35.
8. Ibid., p. 3.
9. Ibid., p. 25.
10. Ibid., p. 17.
11. Ibid., p. 16.
12. Ibid., pp. 198 ss.
13. Ibid., Vol. II, p. 103.
14. Ibid., p. 113.
15. Cf. Ibid., pp. 64 ss.
16. The story is told by Geddes MacGregor, "Introduction to Religious Philosophy," Cambridge, Mass., 1959, p. 17.
17. See for the following: Paul Tillich, "Systematic Theology," Chicago, 1957, Vol. II, pp. 19 ss., and "Theology of Culture," New York, 1959, Chapter VII on "Existential Philosophy: Its Historical Meaning."
18. Albert Camus, "The Fall," London, 1959.
19. Ibid., p. 86.
20. Cf. on this point Dietrich Bonhoeffer's Lectures on "Creation and Fall," London, 1959, which could be called a theological commentary on Camus' book, although Bonhoeffer's book was written about twenty years earlier.
21. Paul Tillich, "The Courage to Be," London, 1955.
22. Paul Tillich, "Theology of Culture," Chapter VIII on "The Theological Significance of Existentialism and Psychoanalysis."
23. Paul Tillich, "Dynamics of Faith," New York, 1957, pp. 16 ss.
24. Paul Tillich, "Systematic Theology," Vol. I, pp. 61, 62.
25. Ibid., Vol. II, p. 15.
26. David Elton Trueblood, "Philosophy of Religion," New York, 1957, pp. 314, 315.
27. Cf. Paul Tillich, "Systematic Theology," Vol. I, pp. 204 ss.
28. Ibid., p. 153 ss.
29. Paul Tillich, "Theology of Culture," Chapter I on "Religion as a Dimension in Man's Spiritual Life."
30. Cf. Paul Tillich, "Systematic Theology," Vol. II, pp. 118 ss.
31. Paul Tillich, "Dynamics of Faith," pp. 1 ss.

32. "The Lost Dimension in Religion," by Paul Tillich, in "Adventures of the Mind,' New York, 1959, p. 55.
33. Paul Tillich, "Dynamics of Faith," pp. 122 ss.
34. Ibid., p. 66.
35. Ibid., p. 124.
36. Ibid., p. 71.
37. H. Thielicke, "Fragen des Christentums an die Moderne Welt," Genf., 1945.
38. Dietrich Bonhoeffer, "Sanctorum Communio," Berlin, 1930.
39. See the personal letters in Dietrich Bonhoeffer, "Gesammelte Schriften," of which three volumes have appeared: Muenchen, Band I, 1958; Band II, 1959; Band III, 1960.
40. Cf. John D. Godsey, "The Theology of Dietrich Bonhoeffer," Philadelphia. Godsey divides Bonhoeffer's life into three stages, marked by Eberhard Bethge's characterizations:
   I   Bonhoeffer said to the theologians: Your theme is the church!
   II Bonhoeffer said to the church: Your theme is the world!
   III Bonhoeffer said to the world: Your theme, forsakenness, is God's own theme!
41. See: Dietrich Bonhoeffer, "Temptation," London, 1956.
42. See: Dietrich Bonhoeffer, "Creation and Fall," London, 1959.
43. Dietrich Bonhoeffer, "Letters and Papers from Prison," Edited by Eberhard Bethge, translated by R. H. Fuller, London, 1954, p. 145.
44. Ibid., p. 146.
45. Loc. cit.
46. Ibid., p. 156.
47. Ibid., p. 147.
48. See Ibid., p. 167.
49. Ibid., p. 154.
50. See Ibid., p. 124, "On the borders it seems to me better to hold our peace and leave the problem unsolved."
51. See Michael B. Foster, "Mystery and Philosophy," London.
52. Dietrich Bonhoeffer, "Letters and Papers from Prison," p. 143.
53. Dietrich Bonhoeffer, "Gesammelte Schriften," Band I, pp. 323 ss.
54. Dietrich Bonhoeffer, "The Cost of Discipleship," London, 1954.
55. Ibid., p. 79.
56. Dietrich Bonhoeffer, "Letters and Papers from Prison," p. 12.
57. Ibid., p. 123.
58. Ibid., p. 122.
59. Ibid., pp. 123, 124.
60. Ibid., p. 142.
61. Ibid., p. 160.
62. See the Poem, "Christians and Unbelievers," Ibid., pp. 166, 167.
63. Ibid., p. 166.
64. Ibid., p. 168.
65. Loc. cit.
66. Ibid., pp. 168, 169.
67. Ibid., p. 139.
68. Dietrich Bonhoeffer, "Life Together," translated by J. W. Doberstein, New York, 1959.
69. Cf. on the Brotherhouse in Finkenwalde, "Gesammelte Schriften," Band II, pp. 448 ss., and Band III, pp. 294 ss.

70. Dietrich Bonhoeffer, "Life Together," p. 77.
71. *Loc. cit.*
72. *Ibid.*, p. 78.
73. Dietrich Bonhoeffer, "Das Gebetbuch der Bibel; Ein Einfuehrung in die Psalmen," Bad Salzuflen, 1955.
74. Dietrich Bonhoeffer, "Life Together," Chapter I on "Community."
75. Emil Brunner, "Die Christliche Lehre von Gott; Dogmatik Band I," pp. 11 ss. and pp. 103 ss.
76. Emil Brunner, "Offenbarung und Vernunft," Zurich, 1941.
77. Emil Brunner, "Die Christliche Lehre von Gott," pp. 109 ss.
78. Emil Brunner, "Man in Revolt; A Christian Anthropology," London, 1947.
79. On the Image of God, see Emil Brunner, "Die Christlich Lehre von Schoepfung und Erloesung; Dogmatik Band II," pp. 64 ss. and 90 ss. Also: Emil Brunner, "Man in Revolt," pp. 91 ss. and 499 ss. Cf. David Cairns, "The Image of God in Man," London, pp. 146 ss.
80. Albert Camus, "The Rebel," translated by A. Bower, New York, 1954.
81. Emil Brunner, "Die Christliche Lehre von Schoepfung und Erloesung," pp. 33 ss., also, "Die Christliche Lehre von Gott," pp. 137 ss. "Man in Revolt," pp. 68 ss. and pp. 527 ss.
82. John Calvin, "Institutes of the Christian Religion," Book I, Ch. VI, 1.
83. Emil Brunner, "Man in Revolt," pp. 237 ss.
84. *Ibid.*, p. 245.
85. *Ibid.*, pp. 527 ss. Also "Die Christliche Lehre von Gott," pp. 107 ss. on "Eristics," Brunner's word for Apologetics.
86. Emil Brunner, "Man in Revolt," p. 536.
87. *Ibid.*, p. 241.
88. Cf. Ian T. Ramsey, "Religious Language," London, 1957.
89. Karl Barth, "Die Lehre von Wort Gottes," Kirchliche Dogmatik I, 2, pp. 304 ss.
90. *Ibid.*, pp. 222 ss. on the Holy Spirit as the subjective reality of Revelation. Cf. also Barth's doctrine of the Trinity in I, 1, pp. 311 ss.
91. Cf. Barth's theological Anthropology in Kirchliche Dogmatik, III, 2, "Die Lehre von der Schoepfung." On the human spirit, pp. 414 ss.
92. Yet he himself gives an excellent "dialogue" with secular anthropologies, *ibid.*, pp. 82 ss.
93. Cf. the article of Yasuo Carl Furuya, on "Apologetic or Kerygmatic Theology?" in "Theology Today," Vol. XVI, Nr. 4, in which he compares the influence and approach of theologians like Tillich and Brunner with that of Barth in Japan.
94. Cf. Barth, Kirchliche Dogmatik I, 2, pp. 28 ss.
95. Rudolf Bultmann, "New Testament and Mythology," p. 5 in "Kerygma and Myth," Ed. by H. W. Bartsch, transl. by R. H. Fuller, London, 1954. Cf. also: R. Bultmann, "Jesus Christ and Mythology," London, 1960.
96. "Kerygma and Myth," p. 1.
97. *Ibid.*, p. 9.
98. *Ibid.*, p. 10.
99. Dorothy Sayers in a letter to average people about Christianity, published by Geddes MacGregor, "Introduction to Religious Philosophy," Cambridge, Mass., p. 11.
100. "Kerygma and Myth," pp. 15 ss.
101. Cf. particularly Bultmann's essay on "The Problem of Hermeneutics," in "Essays Philosophical and Theological," London, 1955, pp. 234 ss.

102. Reinhold Niebuhr, "Essays in Applied Christianity," selected by D. B. Robertson, New York, p. 29.

103. Bultmann himself gives an example of the application of his theological teachings in his sermons: "The World and the Beyond," New York, 1960. The problem in these sermons is not so much what is said as what is not said, e.g. about the Resurrection.

104. On this problem see the excellent discussion on "myth" in Bultmann and in the Bible, in Giovanni Mieggi, "Gospel and Myth in the Thought of Rudolph Bultmann," translated by Bishop Stephen Neill, London, 1960, pp. 91 ss.

105. Cf. Karl Barth, Kirchliche Dogmatik, I, 2, on "Das Wunder der Weihnacht," pp. 187 ss.

106. Albert Camus, "The Fall," London, 1959, pp. 83-85.

107. Cf. Théo Preiss, "The Life in Christ," London, 1952.

108. Oscar Cullmann, "Christus und die Zeit; Die Urchristliche Zeit-und Geschichts-Auffassung," Zurich, 1946, p. 166.